THE STAND & POOR'S GUIDE TO FAIRNESS OPINIONS

PHILIP J. CLEMENTS
PHILIP W. WISLER

McGraw-Hill

New York   Chicago   San Francisco   Lisbon   London   Madrid
Mexico City   Milan   New Delhi   San Juan   Seoul
Singapore   Sydney   Toronto

CONTENTS

Chapter 4

Valuation Methods Employed by Independent Financial Advisors 38

The challenges of serving as an effective fiduciary have never been greater. When transactions enter the picture, the fiduciary's role gets even more challenging. Board members are responsible for evaluating and ultimately approving or rejecting a proposed transaction. Fairness opinions assist board members and other fiduciaries in their evaluations. This book is designed to be a "user's guide" for fiduciaries as they address their duties to the stakeholders of their organizations in utilizing and extracting maximum utility from fairness opinions.

At the turn of the millennium, corporate scandals brought new focus on the importance of fiduciary oversight. The Enron, Tyco, WorldCom, and HealthSouth scandals created new rules, increased SEC and NASD pressure, strengthened constituency advocacy, and expanded the body of jurisprudence affecting board members.

In addition to the succession of corporate scandals, there are other signals that highlight the increased emphasis on and scrutiny of fiduciary oversight. Acquisitions, for example, are frequently used in an attempt to build shareholder value. Unfortunately, acquisitions often do not work. In a study recently published by the *Harvard Business Review*, it was concluded that "70 percent to 80 percent of acquisitions fail," meaning that "they create no wealth for shareholders of the acquiring company." The result was that "takeovers did more damage to investors than did all the dot-coms combined. And while M&A activity has slowed somewhat, it hasn't stopped and never will."[1]

Unless transaction review practices change, ill-prepared fiduciaries will continue to be associated with the destruction of the wealth they have been tasked to protect. Statistics and market commentary such as this emphasize the essential role of prudent and effective board oversight, particularly in the context of transaction review.

Today, the fairness opinion is one of the tools that can be used by the fiduciary to improve the way in which the fiduciary body discharges its duties arising from a proposed transaction. The fairness opinion is an

---

[1] "M&A Needn't Be a Loser's Game," *Harvard Business Review,* June 2003.

independent report on the proposed transaction regarding fairness from a financial point of view. Fairness and related opinions are available to boards for a variety of material corporate events, such as transactions, dividend payments, restructurings, and refinancings. Over the past 20 years, the technical and procedural aspects of preparing and delivering a fairness opinion have evolved substantially. As a result, the fiduciary should seek out the very best technical transaction advice available.

The material in this publication is designed to assist fiduciaries in the process of effectively using a fairness opinion in the course of fulfilling their responsibilities. The courts have had a major influence on the formation of both formal and informal protocols impacting the discharge of fiduciary duties. Where useful, judicial decisions have been incorporated either through reference or more detailed examination.

The discussion proceeds in the following order:

♦ Chapter 1: Role of the fiduciary in the current environment
♦ Chapter 2: Use of a fairness opinion in the decision-making process
♦ Chapter 3: The fairness opinion process
♦ Chapter 4: Valuation methodologies often employed to support the fairness opinion
♦ Chapter 5: Characteristics of good financial projections
♦ Chapter 6: Special situations that may arise in the valuation analysis
♦ Chapter 7: Technical issues that can arise in the fairness opinion process

We hope this publication will prove a useful guide for fiduciaries. Its usefulness will be borne out if the material improves the review process that surrounds material corporate events. Improved rigor and transparency in the evaluation of proposed transactions will invariably lead to better decisions in the pursuit of growth in shareholder value.

CHAPTER 1

The Role of the Fiduciary

Fiduciaries face a shifting legal environment. Constituents are more active. The increased caseload causes the courts to be more active. The regulators and legislators are continuously adjusting the landscape in response to actual and perceived events. At the same time, there is agreement that the fiduciary plays a fundamental part in the functioning of enterprises.

This chapter summarizes the duties that apply to fiduciaries in the exercise of their responsibilities. We will discuss how the use of the fairness opinion reinforces the proper exercise of fiduciary oversight and summarize the types of fiduciaries and constituencies and their roles and interests.

1.1 FIDUCIARY DUTY

1.1.1 Overview

Fiduciaries are charged with the oversight of the organization. They are to protect the assets and safeguard the interests of the constituents. Executing this role involves delegating day-to-day operations to entity leadership and management. At the same time, the fiduciary must ensure that safeguards are in place and be sufficiently active in overseeing management's actions.

The courts define these functions as involving the duty of care and the duty of loyalty. Both of these duties require that a director act in good faith. Several other "duties" and rules are often ascribed to the fiduciary function. In this summary, we will address some of these rules and duties, but these are not always clear-cut since the law of fiduciary responsibility is evolving and reasonably technical. Too often, courts are faced with fact matters that do not fit neatly within the existing law, and the court's opinion tends to muddle the legal framework under which the fiduciary operates. Such rulings make it harder for fiduciaries to know where their responsibilities lie. Thus, legal counsel should be consulted on both the state of the law and its application to the specific facts the fiduciary faces. A full discussion of fiduciary duties is beyond the scope of this material.

1.1.2 Duty of Care

The duty of care requires that fiduciaries act on an informed basis after careful deliberation, and that they exercise the care that an ordinary prudent person would exercise under similar circumstances. Under the duty of care, a fiduciary must act in a diligent and reasonable fashion after due consideration of relevant and adequate information and appropriate deliberations.

The duty of care places an affirmative burden upon the fiduciary to take an active role in the decision process. Failing to become involved, to consider matters of importance, or to make business decisions, may constitute a violation of the duty of care. Courts evaluate the degree to which, prior to making a decision, directors considered all significant information reasonably available to them.

In connection with their decision-making process, directors are entitled to rely upon the reports, opinions, information, and advice of outside advisors. Such advisors must have the requisite degree of professional expertise and must not be subject to any objectionable conflicts of interest.[1] While a board is permitted to use outside advisors to counsel them on significant legal and factual matters affecting their analysis, the board may not delegate its central responsibilities to other decision makers.

The business judgment rule is a defense for the fiduciary when challenged on whether the duty of care has been fulfilled. Under the business judgment rule, the courts are reluctant to second-guess a board's decisions. The business judgment rule forms a rebuttable legal presumption that in making a business decision, the fiduciaries acted on an informed basis, in good faith, and in the honest belief that the action taken was in the best interest of the entity and its constituencies. Normally, an informed decision by a board of directors to take action or not to act is entitled to the business rule presumption.

The use of a fairness opinion by a board speaks to whether the board has fulfilled its duty of care by acting in an informed basis. Fairness opinions have played critical roles in convincing courts that the boards have met their duty of care to shareholders. Unfortunately, the receipt of a fairness opinion does not always demonstrate the exercise of due care. In *Joseph v. Shell Oil Company*[2] and *Weinberger v. UOP, Inc.*,[3] the courts found that the fiduciaries failed to exercise due care even though there were fairness opinions. The courts held that the fairness opinions were invalid due to aggressive time constraints and inadequate information provided to the provider of the fairness opinions.

1.1.3 Duty of Loyalty

The duty of loyalty prohibits unfaithfulness and self-dealing. It requires that board members serve the corporation and its shareholders to the exclusion of all other interests. The duty of loyalty requires the board member to act in a manner reasonably believed to be in the best interest of the corporation. A fiduciary is preferably independent and disinterested. The fiduciary should neither appear on both sides of a transaction nor expect to derive personal financial benefit from it in the sense of self-dealing.

The test of independence focuses on impartiality and objectivity. This test comes into play to determine whether there are any substantial reasons that a director might be incapable of making a decision in only the best interests of the corporation. A fiduciary may be considered compromised by an interest in the transaction if a specific material financial benefit would accrue to the fiduciary as a result of the transaction, or if the fiduciary is beholden to an interested party or decision maker. "Beholden" in this context means not just in the financial sense, but can include other relationships to the interested party.

Directors have generally been considered disinterested despite personal selection by, or relationships with, interested directors. However, these circumstances may factor into the overall judicial analysis of whether a director is found to be independent. A recent Delaware decision[4] suggests that personal and familial ties and other noneconomic factors are very much a part of any independence analysis.

Neither a director's interest as a stockholder, nor an interest in retaining the directorship and the accompanying fees, have caused directors to be deemed interested in a transaction. The receipt of consulting fees paid by the company to a director might raise questions regarding independence where the transaction being contemplated is sponsored by the management of the company.

Where fiduciaries appear on both sides of a challenged transaction, or where the facts support an alleged breach of independence, the court will look to the fiduciary to show that the transaction meets the requirements of "entire fairness." In evaluating the entire fairness of a transaction, the Delaware Supreme Court[5] has stated that "fairness" in this context has two components: "fair dealing" and "fair price." That is, the fairness test is not bifurcated between fair dealing and fair price, but requires that all aspects of the transaction enter the examination to determine entire fairness.

"Fair dealing" embraces procedural matters relating to the timing of the transaction and the way in which the transaction was initiated, structured, negotiated, and disclosed to the directors, and how the approvals of the directors and the stockholders were obtained.[6] In evaluating the fair dealing component of the entire fairness test, courts look at such elements as:

♦ Whether the corporation was financially injured by the timing of the transaction, and at the same time the interested directors personally benefited

♦ Whether the transaction was structured to maximize benefits to the fiduciaries at the expense of corporate profits

♦ Whether the transaction was negotiated by an independent committee of disinterested directors (or otherwise approved by a majority of the disinterested members of the board) or, if stockholder approval is required, whether the transaction was approved by a majority of disinterested stockholders

♦ Whether the directors and, if stockholder approval is required, stockholders were informed of all available material information

The use of a properly functioning committee of disinterested directors to independently assess and negotiate any transaction may help satisfy the fair dealing component and may even shift the burden of proving entire fairness.[7]

"Fair price" looks at all economic and financial matters of the transaction, including market value, earning, assets, future prospects, and any other elements that affect the intrinsic value of a corporation's stock value.

To some extent, the entire fairness test creates uncertainty because it enables a court to substitute its own notions of fairness for that of the board of directors. Careful consideration should be given to the requirement of demonstrating "entire fairness" in connection with any decision to proceed with a transaction.

The duty of loyalty includes the duty of candor,[8] which requires that the board, when seeking stockholder action, disclose fully and fairly pertinent information that a reasonable stockholder would consider material in deciding whether to seek an appraisal, sell the stock, or retain the stock and approve the transaction.

It has been almost two decades since the SEC has proposed new disclosure rules. Recent events and regulatory trends may be a catalyst for new standards in the area of disclosure. In fact, recent cases point to increased duties regarding disclosure and approval of deal price. In *In Re Pure Resources* shareholder litigation,[9] the courts specifically addressed fiduciary responsibilities for disclosure of how the transaction was identified, negotiated, and consummated. In *In Re Mony Group* shareholder litigation,[10] the court reaffirmed the guidance on the fiduciary's role in approving the deal price. In both of these cases, the presence of a fairness opinion was useful in demonstrating that the fiduciaries fulfilled their responsibilities.

At the same time, fiduciaries deal with confidential information. Fiduciaries should deal confidentially with all matters involving the entity that are not publicly disclosed or a matter of public knowledge. No current information regarding corporate or board activities should be discussed with individuals outside the corporation.

1.1.4 Personal Liability

Directors have been held personally liable for decisions that appear hasty, ill considered, or in disregard of significant information. A recent case[11] found that where directors know that they are making material corporate decisions without adequate information or adequate deliberation, such conscious disregard of the directors' duties are either not in good faith or involve intentional misconduct. Such conduct deprives the directors of the business judgment rule protection and subjects the directors to potential liability. (See also the case of *Smith v. Van Gorkom*[12] for the potential of personal liability.) A board should carefully document the basis for its decisions. As noted above, fiduciaries should also adhere to the need for confidentiality, because disclosure of confidential information can cause harm to the entity and be a breach of securities laws, which in turn can lead to personal liability.

Fairness opinions have increasingly been referenced in connection with corporate transaction disputes. During 2003 there were 76 breach of fiduciary duty lawsuits pending in the Delaware Chancery Court. This is more than double the number of pending cases in 2000 and an almost 20 percent increase over 2002. Historical data suggest that the average legal and settlement costs of a lawsuit brought against a director have been estimated at $10 million,[13] and board members may be held personally liable.

Failure of the fiduciary to properly discharge his or her duties has costly implications for the fiduciary, the organization, and the constituency. Costs include damage to stakeholders (including shareholders and creditors) either by paying or receiving too much or too little in a proposed transaction, or by failing to pursue opportunities. The total cost to organizations and their constituencies of deals that were approved based on inadequate or poorly performed due diligence may be beyond reasonable estimation, yet many would immediately recall the often cited 70 to 80 percent nonaccretive track record of M&A deals to reason that this "cost," both in terms of resources and reputations, is huge. In light of the substantial financial and reputation repercussions, the role of the fiduciary cannot be understated.

A fiduciary's role includes the protection of corporate assets, safeguarding the interests of his or her constituents, and active promotion of constituents' interests. Executing this role requires delegation of responsibility to effective management/corporate leadership, while at the same time ensuring that safeguards are in place to constrain board members and management from pursuing self-serving behaviors. Fiduciaries should bear in mind that their duties extend to all stockholders, including those in minority positions.

1.2 THE ACTIVE CONSTITUENCY

In an environment where the subject is contentious, the stakes are high, and heightened regulatory emphasis is placed on independence, transparency, and rigor, it is not surprising that the behavior of the affected constituencies is undergoing its own process of change.

As active supporters of corporate reform, institutional shareholders and consumer activist groups are increasingly vocal and litigious classes of actual and notional constituents. For example, some parties hold that there should be evidence of tension between the board of directors and the management. The absence of this tension has been identified as a recurring characteristic when reviewing the past corporate failures. A *Harvard Business Review* article by Kaufman Montgomery states that, "Directors don't know what shareholders want and shareholders don't know what directors are doing." It goes on to note that, "Transparency and accountability, which rest in the heart of good governance, are essentially missing in [the board member/stakeholder] relationship."[14] Recent court decisions reaffirm the notion that greater transparency should be afforded to stakeholders.[15]

The required improvements in corporate governance, and the SEC's added guidelines regarding adequate disclosure, reinforce the notion that today's constituents expect to see more evidence of the fiduciary's active oversight through both structural changes and increasing documentation. The recent article published in the *Wall Street Journal* titled "NASD Scrutinizes Conflicts in Bankers' Fairness Opinions" articulates the level of constituency concern in the procedures undertaken by the fiduciary and the way this concern is manifesting itself in public inquiry and potential regulation.[16]

The activism is not confined to the relationship between board members and management. There are signs that there is an implicit extension of fiduciary responsibility beyond just the corporate boardroom. For example, fiduciaries were compelled to consider concerns from a coalition of 11 consumer activist groups representing hospitals, health centers, and doctors that opposed the proposed plan of conversion of insurance provider Premera Blue Cross to for-profit status.[17] In this instance, despite the fact that the fiduciaries considered more than 1,200 pages of expert reports, a suit was filed in an attempt to block the conversion, reinforcing the need for fiduciaries to question the impact of their actions on all active constituents.[18]

1.3 NEW FIDUCIARY ROLES

In the past, the fiduciary role was typically viewed as belonging to board members of public and private corporations. The new fiduciary model is much broader and has been expanded to include regulators, legislators, and attorneys general. In many states, legislation has been enacted to give state officials (such as the Attorney General or Department of Insurance) specific transaction oversight where the interests of the state's taxpayers may be involved in a pending transaction. Examples include the sale of a not-for-profit hospital and the conversion of a policyholder-owned insurance company to a stock-based corporation.

In addition, the public accounting reform under the Sarbanes-Oxley Act of 2002, and various proposals and rules for public companies issued by the New York Stock Exchange, the American Stock Exchange, and the Nasdaq, have increased the level of accountability for board members. These initiatives establish new fiduciary requirements, such as the composition and responsibilities of audit committees.

The table below identifies individuals and entities that in some capacity have acted in or may someday be held to the standards of a fiduciary.

Fiduciary	Entity	Overview of Responsibilities
Board of Directors	Independent Subcommittee	Formed to consider specific actions and present findings to the board of directors. The creation of a subcommittee has been viewed by the courts as some evidence of a board carefully administering the duty of care.
	Audit Committee	Usually consists of three or four independent directors. Tasked with assisting the board in its oversight of the integrity of the financial statements; the company's compliance with legal and regulatory requirements; the performance, independence, and qualifications of the company's auditor; and the performance of the company's internal audit function. Under the Sarbanes-Oxley Act, public companies must explain why they do not have at least one financial expert on the audit committee.
	Finance Committee	Usually consists of three independent directors tasked with assisting the board in its oversight of the company's corporate funding policy, securities offerings, budgets and financial objectives, financial commitments, dividends, and related policies.
	Compensation Committee	Usually consists of three independent directors tasked with assisting the board in its overall responsibility relating to senior employee compensation. Often the venue for discussing the use and value of options and other incentive-based compensation schemes.
Board of Trustees	Debt Holders	Tasked with ensuring adequate collateral preservation and meeting debt covenants.
	Not-for-Profit	Responsible for oversight of not-for-profit organizations.
	Mutual Fund Companies	Responsible for oversight of mutual fund companies. Due to recent regulatory reviews, new guidelines are anticipated.
	ESOP Trustees	Responsible for oversight of Employee Stock Ownership Plans.
	Pension Trustees	Responsible for overseeing pension plan assets and meeting retirement obligations.
Regulators	Securities and Exchange Commission	Responsible for fair and equitable securities markets in the United States.

Fiduciary	Entity	Overview of Responsibilities
	Department of Insurance	Responsible for overseeing all registered insurance companies and for granting final approval of the conversion of a mutual insurance company to a stock company. For example, the health care insurance industry has been subject to demutualization and consolidation, which in turn has alerted numerous consumer activists, putting additional pressure on regulators.
	Public Utilities Commission	Responsible for oversight of public utility companies.
	European Trade Commission	Responsible for fair and equitable securities markets in Europe.
Attorneys General	Office of the State Attorney General	Responsible for protection of state citizens and application of state laws, particularly in transactions involving not-for-profit, mutual, and public service organizations.
	Not-for-Profit Regulatory Board	Under various state laws, tasked with oversight of transactions involving charitable and not-for-profit organizations. For example, the Community Health Care Assets Protection Act in New Jersey outlines appropriate steps that the Office of the Attorney General must undertake in its regulatory review of not-for profit health care transactions.
General Trustees	Foundations	Responsible for oversight in accordance with the organization's charter of foundation activities, grants, and capital.
	Charitable Trusts	Responsible for oversight in accordance with the organization's charter of charitable trust activities, grants, and capital.
	Family Trustees	Responsible for oversight in accordance with the organization's charter of family trust activities, grants, and capital.
State Government	State Legislators	Legislators regularly involved in policy formation regarding issues affecting their citizen constituencies.
Federal Government	Federal Legislators	Legislators regularly involved in policy formation regarding issues affecting their citizen constituencies.

Fiduciaries do not typically think of customers, taxpayers, vendors/ suppliers, and employees as members of constituencies to whom the fiduciary body owes a duty (for example, the duty of care and the duty of loyalty), yet these groups often assert themselves as a constituency whose interests should be protected by the fiduciary, and hence be a direct or indirect beneficiary of fiduciary duty. The table below provides a more comprehensive view of the constituencies that either (1) have traditionally benefited by conventional fiduciary protections, or (2) have asserted claims to such protections.

Constituency	Comment
Shareholder (Common Stock)	Well-established corporate and judicial record with regard to the duties owed to this constituency.
Shareholder (Preferred Stock)	Less-established corporate and judicial record with regard to the duties owed to this constituency. The bases of the claims of this group on the corporation are contractual in nature (e.g., certificate of designation or similar instrument spell out the rights and returns associated with this type of investment). When the proposed action may impair the interests of this group, the interests of this class must be considered by the fiduciary.
Option Holder	Similar to preferred stock shareholder.
Creditor (Secured)	Interests of secured creditors are often protected by the terms of the debt instrument employed, thus limiting the duty owed to this class of investor. The instrument may call for a trustee or other separate fiduciary to oversee the bondholder's interest. If the entity is in or near the vicinity of insolvency, the board may owe fiduciary duties to creditors, as well as the entity and its shareholders.
Creditor (Unsecured)	This class relies on their own agreements. The fiduciary overseeing an entity may wish to consider that, under certain transactions, the unsecured creditor might be converted to a notional equity investor in the enterprise. Indeed, if the entity is in or near the vicinity of insolvency, the board may owe fiduciary duties to creditors, as well as the entity and its shareholders.
Vendor (Trade Creditor)	Similar to the unsecured creditor (preceding constituency).
Customer	Typically, only an issue in cooperative or mutual situations. In such instances, a customer may be deemed a notional owner of the enterprise by regulators and legislators as a result of contributions to capital through product pricing, deferred investment returns, and/or lower dividends.
Employee	State and Federal Department of Labor and ERISA regulations set forth rights and claims of this class.
Beneficiaries	Trustees, by virtue of trust agreement and convention, owe duties to the beneficiaries in terms of performance of activities called for under trust documents.

A full discussion of the potential exposure of fiduciaries is beyond the scope of this material, but we have provided a brief bibliography of timely and relevant materials on the topic of Corporate Governance as Appendix I.

NOTES

1. The courts have long accepted that there are acceptable conflicts of interest and that it is nearly impossible to rid a transaction of all conflicts of interest.
2. *Joseph v. Shell Oil Co.*, 482 A.2d 335 (Del. Ch. 1984).
3. *Weinberger v. UOP, Inc.*, 426 A.2d 1333 (Del. Ch. 1981).
4. *In Re Oracle Corp. Derivative Litigation*, 824 A.2d 917 (Del. Ch. 2003).
5. *Weinberger v. UOP, Inc.*, 426 A.2d 1333 (Del. Ch. 1981).
6. See Emerald Partners for a discussion of the elements the courts review in the determination of fair price and fair dealing.
7. For particular types of transactions (e.g., going private transactions), the formation of an independent committee could have other legal implications. The fiduciary body should consult legal counsel.
8. Conceptually described in *Li Second Family Ltd. Partnership v. Toshiba Corp.*, No. 99-1451, 2000 U.S. App. LEXIS 27921 (Fed. Cir. Nov. 8, 2000).
9. *In Re Pure Resources Inc.*, 808 A.2d 421 (Del. Ch. 2002).
10. *In Re Mony Group Inc.*, quoting *McMillan v. Intercargo Corp.*, 768 A.2d 492, 505 n.55 (Del. Ch. 2000).
11. *In Re The Walt Disney Company Derivative Litigation*, 825 A.2d 275 (Del. Ch. 2003).
12. *In Re Mony Group Inc.*, quoting *McMillan v. Intercargo Corp.*, 768 A.2d 492, 505 n.55 (Del. Ch. 2000).
13. "Corporate Governance Review Directors and Officers Liability and Insurance Environment," *National Association of Corporate Directors*, October 31, 1995.
14. Rhonda Kaufman and C. Montgomery, "The Board's Missing Link," *Harvard Business Review*, March 2003.
15. See *Aquila v. Quanta Services, Inc.*, C.A. No. 19497, 805 A.2d 196 (Del. 2002), and *In Re Pure Resources, Inc., Shareholders Litigation*, C.A. No. 19876, 808 A.2d 421 (Del. 2002).
16. Ann Davis, "NASD Scrutinizes Conflicts In Bankers' Fairness Opinions," *Wall Street Journal*, June 11, 2004, 1.
17. Carol Ostrom, "Aid Prospect Draws More Support for Premera Bid; Hearing to Begin on Profit Status," *Seattle Times*, May 3, 2004.
18. Carla Johnson, "Hearing Will Require an Oath; Testimony about Premera Blue Cross Proposal Is Considered Evidence," *Spokesman-Review*, Spokane, Washington, USA, December 2, 2003.

CHAPTER 2

The Role of the Fairness Opinion

This chapter introduces the fairness opinion's uses and limitations, presents an overview of the merits of obtaining a fairness opinion, and discusses some legal perspectives of the fairness opinion.

2.1 WHAT IS A FAIRNESS OPINION?

A fairness opinion is a letter report from a financial advisor to the fiduciaries of an entity contemplating a material transaction. The opinion is addressed to the body charged with the fiduciary duty or regulatory oversight. In it, a qualified financial advisor presents its impartial view of the transaction, which can be relied upon by the fiduciary or regulator as part of the information gathered in its review of the transaction's implications. The independent financial advisor opines on the fairness of the proposed transaction from a financial point of view. A fairness opinion is an expert's judgment; it is not a statement of fact. Ultimately, the fiduciaries have the responsibility of determining whether the action being contemplated is in the best interests of the constituents they represent.

A fairness opinion is more than a typical valuation. It looks at the value of the interests received as compared to the value of the interests given up, and does this in the context of a specific transaction. In addressing the fairness question, value is not so much determined, as it is tested and validated. The hypothetical willing buyer and willing seller in the traditional definition of "fair market value" are actually known in the fairness opinion context. The opinion is developed in response to a specific deal. Many of the techniques used to evaluate a transaction's fairness are similar to the approaches used in valuation generally. However, the particular facts and circumstances of the transaction pose specific valuation problems that must be weighed in the fairness determination.

In addition, fairness opinions require an in-depth assessment of the confidence level of conclusions from the various valuation approaches used within the context of facts and circumstances of the transaction. When undertaking the analysis, the independent financial advisor is cognizant of potential trade-offs between accuracy and confidence. The range of values is developed and tested by reference to a series of possible outcomes (positive and negative) that could affect value. In contrast, a typical valuation considers the various approaches in an attempt to identify a specific point estimate.

A straightforward application for fairness opinions would be the fairness of a cash price to the seller of a wholly owned business. If the price is within the range of values for the business under likely scenarios, the transaction would be deemed fair from a financial point of view. Barring any uniqueness in the business, determining its value would be a straightforward exercise.

To illustrate the complexities in the fairness opinion analysis, consider a private buyer paying a premium for a public company and including its own equity in the transaction consideration. In this case, the valuation exercise becomes more complex because the analysis has to consider the private company's equity value and the strategic and synergistic rationale for a premium. In looking at the value of the public company, the trading characteristics of the market price would require analysis (i.e., is the market pricing rational and fully informed?).

Due to the assumption sets employed, a fairness opinion is valid only for a specific point in time and is typically subject to the assumptions and limitations disclosed in the opinion.

There are a number of things a fairness opinion does not do. For instance, it does not cover certain aspects of a transaction that the fiduciary may wish to review and for which the fiduciary may seek out other opinions (i.e., technology compatibility for a software developer). Also, the fairness opinion is not an assurance that the best possible price or terms have been achieved. Typically, it is not an affirmation of the sale or negotiation process, does not attest to the effectiveness of any auction process, and is not an evaluation of the strategic merit of the transaction, beyond those necessary to address the valuation analysis in the opinion. Further, to the extent that there are related parties in the transaction, the fairness opinion does not typically address the question of fair dealing; the legal ramifications of a transaction are not attested; and the fairness opinion is not an audit or attestation of the financial results, historic or prospective.

2.2 SPECIFIC FUNCTIONS OF A FAIRNESS OPINION

The fairness opinion has three uses in a contemplated transaction: (1) aiding fiduciaries in the decision-making process, (2) mitigating fiduciaries' risk, and (3) enhancing communications regarding the soundness of a contemplated action.

2.2.1 Aiding in Decision Making

An independent view of the contemplated transaction using a well-supported, robust, and credible analysis is a valuable resource to fiduciaries in the decision-making process. Where there is no credible market pricing mechanism or auction process to validate pricing, boards and fiduciaries should be particularly concerned about validating recommendations of management or other interested parties. Fairness opinions are particularly helpful in these cases.

If the business contemplating a sale has recently experienced poor performance, for example, the board could request that the analysis for the fairness opinion include a scenario analysis modeling whether it would be more beneficial to wait for the business to turn around. This analysis would provide the board with an alternative perspective relative to the offer on the table.

2.2.2 Mitigating Risk

Fairness opinions mitigate risk by providing evidence that the board exercised due care in its deliberations on a proposed transaction by obtaining the opinion of an independent financial advisor. *Deal Makers Journal* noted, " . . . the Enron scandal has increased the urgency with which boards have sought out the financial backstopping that a fairness opinion provides."[1]

A word of caution: Fiduciaries often rely on fairness opinions rendered by the financial advisors (i.e., investment banks) who conceived of the deal or managed the transaction process. Usually, the financial advisor's transaction fees are paid only if the transaction is completed. Recent cases and regulatory activity are bringing into question the financial advisor's potential conflict of interest, and thereby the merit of their fairness opinions. This is discussed in more detail in Section 3.3.5.

2.2.3 Enhancing Communication

The fairness opinion can be used to enhance the communications to stakeholders that the fiduciaries have exercised due care and acted independently and objectively. The level and form of disclosure is receiving increased attention due to the presumption that the communication of an independent financial advisor's opinion on the adequacy of the price has a material impact on the decision of shareholders to tender shares or to approve a transaction. The Securities and Exchange Commission does require fairness opinions to be included in proxy statements under Item 8 of SEC Schedule 13E-3 (provided in Appendix II). See Section 2.4 below for additional discussion regarding disclosure requirements.

All of these functions have caused the fairness opinion to take on more importance. The receipt of a fairness opinion should not be an afterthought.

2.3 WHEN SHOULD A FIDUCIARY SEEK A FAIRNESS OPINION?

Historically, fairness opinions have been used by fiduciaries of sellers, buyers, and joint venture partners. More recently, legislators, regulators, consumer groups, and other interested parties are seeking fairness opinions or similar analysis as a means of increasing their understanding of how a transaction affects their interests. Today, fairness opinions are used by fiduciaries in their review of:

- Mergers and acquisitions
- Tender offers, particularly those involving the buyout of minority shareholders
- Private placements
- Management buyouts
- Corporate restructuring (including going private, or de-listing; demutualization; and conversion from not-for-profit to for-profit transactions)
- Loan covenant requirements

They are also used by fiduciaries when requested by regulators, such as state attorneys general, state insurance commissioners, and public utility commissions.

2.4 DISCLOSURE REQUIREMENTS FOR FAIRNESS OPINIONS

The Securities and Exchange Commission continues to develop new rules and proposals to improve disclosure. The primary objective of the initiatives being undertaken by the SEC is to "bring everyone back to a sense of business integrity."[2] The new rules are designed to improve the timing and depth of public disclosure and to enhance the corporate governance process.

The level of detail in public disclosure has been expanded to include sufficient information to enable the stakeholders to reach their own conclusions on value for the subject company. As of the printing of this users' guide, the rules have not been finalized, but it is expected that future proxy statements will be required to disclose:

- An overview of the transaction, including deal structure, merits of the transaction, and a chronology of events leading up to the transaction
- An outline of the alternatives to the transaction that were considered by the fiduciaries, including terms of other transactions
- A statement from the fiduciaries regarding whether they believe the transaction is fair or unfair to the unaffiliated securities holders
- A discussion on the factors the fiduciaries considered in reaching their conclusion regarding the question of fairness

The SEC has also improved its proxy statement review process by moving away from sampling techniques, reviewing statements in more detail, asking more questions, and providing more comments. In the past, such scrutiny was typically reserved for going private transactions.

NOTES

1. "Fairness Opinions Come to the Fore," *Mergers & Acquisitions: The Dealmakers Journal* 37.5, May 2002: 16.
2. Amy Borrus, "The SEC's Top Cop Means Business," *BusinessWeek,* June 23, 2003.

CHAPTER 3

Fairness Opinion Process

This chapter provides an overview of the process for selecting an independent financial advisor and the process for rendering a fairness opinion.

3.1 FIDUCIARY PROCESS

Once the fiduciary is alerted to the prospect of a material transaction, it should, with the guidance of counsel, determine the merit of (1) establishing or commissioning its own transaction advisory committee (e.g., committee of independent board members, audit committee, finance committee) whose mandate includes transaction evaluation and recommendations to the board, and (2) retaining an independent financial advisor to render a fairness opinion in connection with the proposed transaction.

3.1.1 Use of an Independent Committee

The use of an independent committee has been found to be a prudent step. This is true particularly in circumstances where related parties may be involved in the proposed transaction or when board members have meaningful economic positions in some element of the proposed transaction.

Concurrent with efforts to appoint an independent financial advisor, the fiduciary should determine whether it needs to set up its own independent committee to oversee the transaction review process. Independent committees are often used to make recommendations to the fiduciary body; however, in most instances the fiduciary body still retains ultimate responsibility for fulfilling its duties. Independent committees (which can include the organization's audit committee) are often comprised of individuals who have no conflict of interest related to the proposed transaction and who bring the necessary skills to the table in order to make an informed recommendation.

The Delaware courts have noted that an independent committee must be "independent in fact . . . energetic, informed and well motivated."[1] In light of this, the independent committee's authority in evaluating the proposed transaction should be clear from the outset and not unduly limited. This authority should include the power to determine whether or not to proceed with the proposed transaction, as well as the power—should a decision be made to proceed—to negotiate the price.

In addition to being independent in composition, the committee must act independently. Thus, the independent committee should bear in mind that the courts, which may review the decision to move forward with or reject the proposed transaction, will focus on the process undertaken and the negotiation of the transaction. Specifically, the courts will be looking to see that the independent committee, *inter alia*:

1. Engages in a thorough analysis of the proposed transaction (including a determination whether it is in the best interest of the corporation)
2. Proactively reviews the work of its independent financial advisors (e.g., by asking questions of its advisors and staying well-informed throughout the process)
3. Proactively negotiates
4. Keeps the board informed of what is happening during the course of its evaluation

The independent committee should devote an adequate amount of time to its analysis of the proposed transaction, and any related analysis and discussion by an independent committee should be well documented (i.e., evidence of some discussions on this topic should be reflected in the independent committee's minutes). The independent committee should also take care to avoid participation by the interested party in the independent committee's deliberative process.

The independent committee should choose its own financial advisors without the involvement of the interested directors. Financial advisors who have a relationship with the interested director(s) may lack the requisite independence to serve as advisors for the independent committee. The Delaware courts have noted that "[a] suspicious mind is made uneasy contemplating the possibilities when the interested CEO is so active in choosing his adversary."[2]

The independent committee should retain its own independent financial advisors to assist in determining a fair price and fair structure for any potential transaction.

Should a recommendation be made to the board, the board should likewise devote adequate time to the review of the independent committee's work and consideration of any recommendation from the independent committee.

While, strictly speaking, an independent committee may not be necessary if a majority of the directors on the board appear to be disinterested and independent, an independent committee could shift the burden of persuasion if any board decision to move forward with, or reject, the proposed transaction faces a subsequent challenge requiring the board to prove the entire fairness of any decision. In the event that an independent committee is not utilized, any director who is not disinterested or independent should abstain from discussions and votes taken relating to the proposed transaction. In addition, the retention of independent, outside financial advisors is critical with respect to the process in all events.

Once again, the focus will be on the process followed by the board in making its decision: The board should, *inter alia*, engage in a thorough analysis of the proposed transaction, proactively review the work of its independent financial advisors, and proactively negotiate transaction terms.

3.1.2 Selection of an Independent Financial Advisor

The fiduciary or the independent committee may desire an independent financial advisor's opinion on the merits of a proposed transaction. The retention of an independent financial advisor may involve a proposal process to determine the merits and relative strengths of different experts. Senior management, in-house or outside counsel, or board members may recommend potential independent financial advisors. Concerns over the timing and confidentiality in the transaction process have often been cited by fiduciaries to forego the request-for-proposal process. However, requests for proposal are often the best way to surface the most qualified, independent financial advisor.

The choice of an independent financial advisor can be as important as the opinion itself. The answers to the following questions can help direct the fiduciary to a well-reasoned choice:

+ Can the financial advisor be perceived as having a conflict of interest?
+ Can the financial advisor be regarded as having the best interests of the client in mind?
+ Has the financial advisor demonstrated the requisite valuation expertise, industry knowledge, and relevant experience?

• Does the financial advisor have the reputation and resources to support the opinion?

• Has the financial advisor ever received criticism in the courts or the press for prior fairness opinions?

• Does the financial advisor have the resources to meet the time constraints imposed by transaction deadlines and deal participants?

"Fiduciary responsibility necessitates looking closely at the webs of conflicting interests among accountants, auditors . . . investment bankers . . . and boards."[3] In the past, the deal advisor—usually the board's investment banker—rendered a high percentage of fairness opinions. The contingent nature of deal advisor compensation arrangements typically used by investment banks is cited as a potential conflict of interest. New York Attorney General Eliot Spitzer has publicly questioned investment banks providing fairness opinions on mergers and acquisitions and has encouraged federal regulators—most notably the SEC—to look into the independence of opinions rendered by an advisor whose primary fees are contingent on deal completion.[4]

The NASD is also considering the implications of investment bank involvement in both transaction advisory and fairness opinion services on the same transaction.[5] In the future, pressure may be brought to bear by federal regulators to mandate that compensation arrangements be disclosed or that fiduciaries use an independent financial advisor for a fairness opinion. The *Dealmakers Journal* states that, "One advantage of using an independent financial advisor . . . [is that the advisor is] less likely to be conflicted than the bulge-bracket investment banks."[6]

Under certain circumstances, it may be prudent for the fiduciary to engage two separate independent financial advisors, one to write the fairness opinion with an appropriate fee structure, but not a contingency fee, and one to provide transaction advisory services the company's board or management may require, with an appropriate fee structure, which may be a contingency fee. With such an approach, the fiduciary may have a better case to present in the event its role in the transaction approval process comes under judiciary scrutiny.

A board faces a challenge in obtaining an independent fairness opinion from an institution of scale and stature that has not provided transaction advisory services. This proves difficult when most investment banks will not render a fairness opinion on a transaction they did not lead. The exception is for very large clients or transactions where in-house teams did the deal. An example is the Disney-ABC/CapCities transaction, where both sides used in-house teams to negotiate the deal terms. Each then brought in their investment banker to render a fairness opinion. In that instance, the only fees to investment bankers for deal advice were for the fairness opinions.

Other independent financial advisors have begun to provide fairness opinions, but during the 1990s some withdrew. Large accounting firms rendered fairness opinions in the past, but have since constrained their activities in this area due to auditor independence issues. Most of the independent fairness opinion providers are smaller investment banks and independent valuation firms.

Too often the determining factor in selecting an independent financial advisor is price. The amount of the fee is certainly relevant, but the old adage, "You get what you pay for," can be seen in recent cases. Fiduciaries should look for independent financial advisors who can help them exercise their responsibilities in an insightful and objective manner. The expertise should always be the most important selection criteria.

Fee estimates—preferably fixed in nature and not tied to a specific transaction outcome—will vary greatly, depending on a variety of transaction-specific factors that can include, but are not limited to, the following transaction characteristics:

- ♦ Materiality of the proposed transaction
- ♦ Scope of analysis
- ♦ Status of the business or assets purchased or sold (e.g., start-up, mature business, stand-alone assets/intellectual property, bundled going concern, multinational, multi-industry, holding/portfolio company, wholly owned, fractional ownership, etc.)
- ♦ Data quality and quantity (may require financial advisors to perform additional analysis to corroborate data and assumptions)
- ♦ Level of transaction complexity (e.g., presence of earn-outs, contingent payments)
- ♦ Form of consideration paid or received
- ♦ Breadth of distribution/reliance on findings

Each of the foregoing characteristics impacts on the advisors' development of a confidence interval around the transaction economics, and depending on the circumstances, can only be addressed through incremental analysis and investment of time and resources. In the event that there is material disparity between fee estimates from advisors, the fiduciary should attempt to ensure that the advisors have factored in all relevant facts in developing their estimates, giving consideration to the list of transaction characteristics highlighted above.

A key concern of the fiduciary following the selection process should be the independent financial advisor's commitment to, and process for, early identification and communication of any material deal issues encountered once work has begun. Attention to, and prior experience with, this aspect of project communication is essential to identifying and recommending solutions for transaction and pricing issues in an orderly manner.

In the event that an independent committee is established, an important outcome of the initial discussions with the independent financial advisor will be to clarify whether the fiduciary body or its independent committee will be the recipient of the opinion and the independent financial advisor's presentation of findings.

3.1.3 Other Considerations

Hiring an independent financial advisor does not relieve the fiduciaries of their responsibilities to investigate all available information before a transaction. Rather, fiduciaries are required to read, understand, and challenge the methods, assumptions, and conclusions supporting the opinion of an independent financial advisor before relying on such an opinion.

Central to the transaction review process is allowance for sufficient time to develop and thoughtfully consider transaction issues and economics. A word of caution: Courts have been critical of fiduciaries that have failed to insist on sufficient time to thoughtfully consider the recommendations of management and independent financial advisors engaged specifically for the purpose of validating the transaction's terms. The *Great Western*[7] court decision demonstrated that the execution of an agreement to sell the company is not the end of the road, but rather, that the directors' fiduciary duties remain in place until consummation of a transaction.

Finally, to extract greatest value from the process, the fiduciary should ensure that the independent financial advisor has open access to all relevant information, management, and third-party advisors.

3.2 INDEPENDENT FINANCIAL ADVISOR PROCESS

The independent financial advisor's process must be rigorous, thorough, and defensible in order to give the fiduciary body confidence in the opinion. Evidence of such a process is essential to establishing a reasonable basis for reliance and reliability in the results of the independent financial advisor. Processes vary from advisor to advisor.

FIGURE 3-1

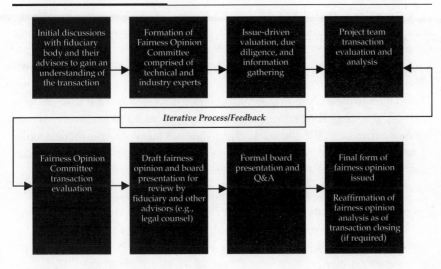

The Standard & Poor's Corporate Value Consulting (CVC) process is presented as an illustration (Figure 3-1).

The following sections outline each of the steps illustrated in the above figure.

3.2.1 Initial Discussions with the Fiduciary

Once engaged, the project team meets with the fiduciary to review the nature of the transaction, discuss particular concerns that the fiduciary may have, review the timing of the transaction, and discuss the roles of both the independent financial advisor and the fiduciary. The project team is available to discuss any concerns the fiduciary may have.

3.2.2 The Fairness Opinion Committee

S&P CVC establishes its own Fairness Opinion Committee for every fairness opinion assignment. The Fairness Opinion Committee is the issuing body for the fairness opinion, rather than any individual. This committee oversees the work of the project team, and is responsible for providing guidance on areas to expand the analysis, challenge the methodologies and assumptions employed, and ascertain the reasonableness of the preliminary value indications.

The Fairness Opinion Committee will seek the advice of its own counsel on legal matters ranging from engagement acceptance to the ultimate form of the opinion rendered. A feature of the Fairness Opinion Committee process is the ability to caucus confidentially with both internal and outside advisors relative to the transaction analysis and advice provided to the fiduciary.

The Fairness Opinion Committee is comprised of technical experts with experience in the process of rendering fairness opinions, professionals with experience in the industry, and professionals with transaction skills or financial insights to assist in the evaluation of the proposed financial arrangements. The Fairness Opinion Committee members bring:

1. Industry insight (i.e., knowledge of appropriate industry-specific valuation multiples, market dynamics, value drivers, etc.)
2. Ability to address anticipated technical issues such as:
   - Capital structure complexities
   - Tax structures
   - Accounting conventions
3. Extensive experience in the application of the methodologies to be employed, such as:
   - Valuation and corporate finance techniques
   - Uncertainty modeling and simulation (e.g., Monte Carlo simulation)
   - Binomial option pricing and derivatives analysis
   - Real Options analysis
   - Robust revenue projection (particularly in the case of start-up ventures or the transfer of nascent intellectual property)
4. Relevant qualifications and credentials (i.e., CFA, CPA, Ph.D., MBA)

In matters beyond the level of expertise of the project team or Fairness Opinion Committee, guidance will be sought from third parties.

Once formed, the Fairness Opinion Committee is briefed by the project team and begins to provide guidance on technical issues and industry value drivers.

3.2.3 Information Gathering and Valuation Due Diligence

The project team gathers information, completes valuation due diligence, and performs the necessary analytics.

The team will interview key members of management and third-party advisors in order to gain a detailed understanding of the elements of the proposed transaction. An information request list will most likely be submitted to the fiduciary (or management) that outlines specific financial and other information needs. Appendix III provides a representative information request list that may be issued in connection with a fairness opinion project. The team will ask management or the entity to represent that the information given is complete and accurate. The fiduciary must understand the extent to which the independent financial advisor has relied on information provided by management.

The project team will review the due diligence done by the entity, as well as the assumptions and strategy of management. The team should review the interests and transaction implications on various parties to the transaction. The investigations conducted by the project team do not replace or duplicate the financial, operating, and legal due diligence performed by the company and its other advisors but may benefit from the knowledge gained as a result of these efforts. Rather, the project team focuses primarily on value drivers in the business and validation of pro forma historical and prospective operating results.

The project team will perform independent research in order to gain insights into the market, industry, and position of the subject company, and the potential implications of the proposed transaction.

3.2.4 Transaction Evaluation

After gathering adequate information, the project team identifies a list of issues and areas of concern with the proposed transaction. Different parties may have special interests to be considered. Facets of the transaction may require further clarification. Assumptions are compared to industry trends for validation.

The project team builds valuation models for the various components of the proposed transaction. These models need to be flexible enough to handle changes that may happen during the final transaction negotiation process. The analysis incorporates key assumptions and value drivers identified and validated by the team during due diligence. From this analysis, the team should have a preview of the values of the entities and the value implications of the proposed transaction.

Once the project team has performed its preliminary analysis, it will present its findings to the Fairness Opinion Committee. In this review, the Fairness Opinion Committee affirms their understanding of the terms of the proposed transaction and the potential issues that may arise from those terms from a fairness perspective. The value analysis framework is reviewed for technical accuracy and assumptions are corroborated. The Fairness Opinion Committee identifies follow-up issues and areas of concern for the fiduciary. In addition, the committee addresses any scope limits on the analysis and data gathering.

The outcome of this presentation results in an iterative process whereby the project team will be tasked to perform further analysis in specific areas and then follow-up with the Fairness Opinion Committee on the outcome of such analysis.

In addition to the internal dialogue with the Fairness Opinion Committee, the project team will concurrently confirm information, assumptions, and representations made by the company and management in connection with the initial transaction analysis.

3.2.5 Preparation of Draft Fairness Opinion

Once the Fairness Opinion Committee is satisfied with the analysis and is confident that the proposed transaction is fair, a draft fairness opinion and a draft presentation for the attention of the fiduciary are prepared. In most instances, these documents are reviewed by the fiduciaries' legal counsel prior to being submitted to the fiduciary for review. This step is a professional courtesy designed to avoid potential last-minute discussion over the form and substance of the opinion or presentation. Provision of these documents does not constitute a formal conclusion that the transaction is fair.

At this juncture, the fiduciary is informed as to whether the proposed transaction will be found to be fair. The presentation of preliminary findings to the fiduciary is critical to the process. The fiduciary must review these findings thoroughly to ensure that all insights of the project team are considered. The project team should be able to address open issues or concerns of the fiduciary. Any limitations on the project team's scope are presented to the fiduciary. Such limitations may lead to qualifications in the independent financial advisor's opinion, and therefore, the fiduciary should be intimate with these limitations. Failure to understand the extent of these limitations may result in a failure on the part of the fiduciary to fulfill his or her duty of care.

In the event that the Fairness Opinion Committee determines that a fairness opinion cannot be issued on the proposed transaction, this does not necessarily mean that the deal is unfair. Rather, the committee has concluded that the available analysis is insufficient to generate confidence that the proposed transaction is fair. In cases where the independent financial advisor does not have enough confidence to render a fairness opinion, the fiduciary may elect to:

1. Request the independent financial advisor to stand down and not issue an opinion
2. Request the independent financial advisor to issue an opinion stating that the transaction cannot be supported within a reasonable range of confidence from a financial point of view
3. Renegotiate the terms of the transaction

The project team may also assist in the drafting of disclosure language related to its opinion and analysis for inclusion in formal filings related to the transaction, e.g., proxy statements. This is done at the draft opinion stage, early enough in the process so that changes in the transaction, issues, and assumptions can be accepted.

3.2.6 Fairness Opinion Committee Approval

As the transaction moves through the formal approval process, and the time to issue the fairness opinion draws near, the Fairness Opinion Committee performs its final review of the terms of the transaction, the analysis of the transaction, and the basis for the opinion. Any open issues are resolved. Each member of the Fairness Opinion Committee must affirm and certify that he or she is confident that the transaction is fair from a financial point of view. The committee then approves the issuance of the opinion.

3.2.7 Formal Board Presentation

After the Fairness Opinion Committee approves the issuance of the fairness opinion, but prior to the issuance, the project team will present its findings to the fiduciary. The presentation will contain the final valuation indications, the assumptions, the value drivers, and the rationale for the fairness opinion. Because the fiduciary has the ultimate responsibility for determining the fairness of, and approving, the proposed transaction, all outstanding issues should be discussed and resolved by the fiduciary and project team during this session or subsequent meetings, if required. This step should be completed proximate to the meetings held to discuss and approve the proposed transaction.

3.2.8 Fairness Opinion Issuance

The fairness opinion is effective as of a specific date and is therefore typically issued proximate to the date that final transaction deliberations are being conducted. The fairness opinion is issued at the end of the deal process, because it is an assessment of the actual deal being done. In transactions with lengthy regulatory or stakeholder approval processes, several months may elapse between the date a transaction is approved by the fiduciary body and (1) the date the transaction is voted on by shareholders and/or (2) the date the transaction actually closes. Legal counsel often advises the fiduciary to seek a written reaffirmation of the opinion at closing.

All of the materials and schedules prepared by the independent financial advisor remain the advisor's property. It is up to the discretion of the independent financial advisor what materials, if any, are shared with the fiduciary. In order for the advisor to develop a truly independent and rigorous analysis, the independent financial advisor needs to retain the ability to confer and deliberate in confidence.

3.3 SOME LEGAL PERSPECTIVES ON THE PROCESS

Observing the repercussions of poorly executed transaction review is instructive for both the fiduciary and the independent financial advisor. To this end, several cases are explored in the next sections that illustrate the risk of emphasizing form over substance in performing the transaction review process. These cases highlight the need for:

1. A well-executed review process by the financial advisor (*M&F Worldwide v. Perelman*)
2. A well-executed review process by the fiduciary (*Smith v. Van Gorkom [Trans Union]*)
3. Rigorous analytical support (*Hanson Trust PLC v. ML SCM Acquisition*)
4. Fiduciary independence (*Howard v. Shay*)
5. Advisor independence (*Smith v. Shell Petroleum, Inc.*)

3.3.1 A Case to Set the Stage: *M&F Worldwide v. Perelman*[8]

Background

Ronald Perelman controlled both Panavision, a manufacturer of sophisticated film and film editing equipment, and M&F Worldwide, a manufacturer of licorice and other flavoring extracts. In 2001, M&F Worldwide acquired a controlling interest in Panavision. The deal pricing of $17.50 per share constituted a 400 percent premium over Panavision's prevailing trading price, and a valuation of approximately 13 times Earnings Before Interest Taxes Depreciation and Amortization (EBITDA). Panavision, for the 2000 fiscal year, had achieved Earnings Before Interest and Taxes (EBIT) of $30.8 million with interest expense of $48.6 million on $500 million of interest bearing debt. Standard & Poor's Ratings had given the target's debt a junk rating. The M&F Worldwide board's advisor, Houlihan Lokey, developed a range of value for the acquired shares of $9.10 to $20.50 per share.

M&F Worldwide shareholders pursued legal action against the board based on their concern with the substance of the transaction. The shareholders' claim stated that " . . . some or all of the transactions entered into were (i) unfair to M&F Worldwide and its shareholders, (ii) constituted corporate waste and mismanagement, and (iii) represented a breach by the Defendants of their fiduciary duties of care, loyalty, and good faith despite the fact that the Defendant(s) formed an independent committee to consider the deal." The shareholders of M&F Worldwide asserted that the board and its advisor significantly overvalued the target. Furthermore, the M&F shareholders asserted that the board's advisor performed little or no due diligence regarding the financial projections it had been given by management. [9]

Litigation Outcome

The M&F Worldwide class action suit was settled on July 26, 2002, effectively unwinding all aspects of the deal. All consideration paid was returned and meaningful litigation costs were incurred. The court criticized the board and Houlihan Lokey for the conclusions reached and opinions issued to M&F Worldwide.

Lesson Learned

This case provides an example of the pitfalls of ignoring classic warning signals in proposed transactions (see Appendix IV for a list of due diligence questions typically posed in an effort to disclose warning signs in transactions). The fact that there was little evidence of a sound business rationale for the acquisition (i.e., business synergy in products or services, complimentary customer list, back office consolidation opportunities, scale benefits), combined with the fact that a significant premium was being paid—both in terms of the purchase price expressed as a multiple of earnings and the proposed share price as a percentage of current trading value—provided strong and early indications that the transaction had potential fairness issues.

To better assure fiduciary independence, the board may need to establish an independent committee to review the proposed transaction. Independent board members should be involved with the decision, and they may require the benefit of their own counsel throughout the process. A sound process employed by the board, the independent committee, and the advisor may question the business rationale and pricing of the deal and thereby strengthen the fiduciary process undertaken to review the proposed transaction, the structure of the deal, and the underlying valuation.

3.3.2 A Case for Process:
Smith v. Van Gorkom (Trans Union)[10]

Background
In the late 1970s, Trans Union, a publicly traded diversified holding company with principal earnings from a rail-car leasing business, sought out potential mergers in an attempt to increase their taxable income to manage a significant tax credit and address other cash flow problems.

At the time, Jerome Van Gorkom (Chairman of Trans Union) determined that $55 a share would be an appropriate price to sell Trans Union in the event of a potential merger, without any financial justification or independent financial advisor opinion on value. Van Gorkom subsequently met with Jay Pritzker, a takeover specialist with the Marmon Group, which was interested in acquiring Trans Union. On September 5, 1980, Van Gorkom held a meeting with the board of directors of Trans Union to discuss a merger with Pritzker. Only two of the nine board members who voted supported the proposed transaction. At no point in these deliberations did the board of directors discuss the methodology, or lack thereof, for supporting a share price of $55 representing a control premium of 48 percent over the market price.

Subsequently, on September 19, 1980, Van Gorkom held an extraordinary meeting to vote on the proposed transaction. At this meeting, Trans Union's attorneys informed the board of directors that a fairness opinion was not necessary to approve the proposed transaction and that they could be sued by shareholders if they did not accept the proposed terms. Trans Union's investment bankers, Salomon Brothers, were not present at this meeting, and none of the board members had a strong financial background. Based exclusively on Van Gorkom's oral presentation, the board of directors made the decision to accept the merger proposal from Pritzker at $55 per share.

Senior management threatened to resign when the transaction was announced. In an effort to appease management, Van Gorkom attempted to restructure the merger agreement with Pritzker, and Salomon Brothers attempted to solicit other offers for a period of 90 days. However, Van Gorkom did not realize that several additional stipulations put into the contract by Pritzker made it very difficult for any other firm to compete with Pritzker. Ultimately, all outstanding shares were sold to Pritzker after a shareholders vote based on limited information.

Following the consummation of the transaction, a class action lawsuit was filed by shareholders against the board of directors. The question that arose before the court was "whether the directors have informed themselves prior to making a business decision of all information reasonably available to them." It is important to note that at no point were the intentions of the board questioned. It is believed that they acted in good faith and with the best of intentions; furthermore, $55 per share, which was a 48 percent premium over the market price, appeared to be more than fair. Nonetheless, this was not the question before the court. Rather, the court was tasked with determining whether the board of directors acted based on a credible transaction review process.

Litigation Outcome

In its defense, Van Gorkom argued that the board of directors utilized the business judgment rule because they were highly qualified to make such a decision, were well informed as to the current position of Trans Union, and had discussed the merger on three separate occasions, thus exercising due diligence. The court disagreed with this position, stating that the board's actions showed "gross negligence" given that it was not well informed and did not question the methodology utilized by Van Gorkom in determining the transaction price. Furthermore, the court concluded that Van Gorkom's attempts to alter the merger proposal were "ineffectual," and that the board failed in performing their duty of full disclosure by not presenting shareholders with all relevant information pertaining to the deal.

Lesson Learned

In order to avoid criticism, the fiduciary and the independent financial advisor should ensure that they undertake a credible review process in connection with a proposed transaction. The business judgment rule includes a requirement to make informed decisions, such that a fiduciary would be better protected if they receive, and have time to consider, independent reports, such as a fairness opinion.

3.3.3 A Case for Rigor:
Hanson Trust PLC v. ML SCM Acquisition[11]

Background

SCM was a New York–based chemicals, coatings, resins, paper products, consumer foods, and pigments business. In the mid 1980s the pigments and consumer foods segments were considered to be SCM's most valuable operations.

On August 21, 1985, Hanson Trust PLC announced a hostile takeover bid for SCM Corp., offering a $60 per share cash tender offer for all outstanding shares of SCM common stock. Subsequently, SCM management met with their investment bank, Goldman Sachs, to discuss a response to Hanson's bid and possible options to avoid a hostile takeover. Goldman Sachs suggested looking for a potential "white knight" or a possible leveraged buyout. After some exploration, Goldman Sachs was unable to find any potential "white knights"; however, Merrill Lynch showed interest in a leveraged buyout.

Merrill Lynch made an official offer for a leveraged buyout ultimately equating to $70 per share. Goldman Sachs informed SCM's board of directors that $70 per share was a fair price. However, Goldman conducted no valuation analysis, provided no report supporting this price, and no member of the SCM board asked for such a report. Consequently, Hanson raised their tender offer to $72, followed by Merrill, which eventually offered $74 for a leveraged buyout. However, the Merrill Lynch offer included several other provisions. Specifically, under a "lockup option" Merrill Lynch would "have the irrevocable right to purchase SCM's pigments business for $350,000,000 and SCM's Durkee Famous Foods for $80,000,000 in the event that a third party acquired more than one-third of SCM's common stock."

SCM's board of directors held a meeting to decide whether to accept Merrill's proposed buyout. Goldman Sachs was present at this meeting and advised the board that $74 per share was a fair price and stated that the asset lockup option was "within the range of fair value," although Goldman never stated what that fair range was. It was later established that Goldman Sachs also failed to perform a valuation analysis to support the value of SCM's pigments and Durkee Famous Foods business divisions implied by the "lockup option." The SCM board of directors simply accepted Goldman Sachs' word without investigating whether there was any sound financial analysis underlying Goldman's assessment of what was a "fair" price. The board of directors accepted Merrill's offer.

Following the signing of the option lockup agreement, Hanson PLC, which was also a shareholder of SCM, filed suit against the SCM board, claiming "SCM directors failed adequately to inform themselves under the duty of care."

Litigation Outcome
The U.S. Court of Appeals maintained that the directors had an obligation to rigorously evaluate the methodologies, assumptions, and supporting documentation used by their financial advisor; in this case, Goldman Sachs. Although the appellate court agreed with the district court's findings that there was no fraud, bad faith, or self-dealing committed by SCM's directors, it stated that the inquiry into their acts is not shielded by the business judgment rule when their "methodologies and procedures" were "so restricted in scope, so shallow in execution, or otherwise so pro forma or half-hearted as to constitute a pretext or sham."[12]

Lesson Learned
Fiduciaries are required to rigorously analyze and inspect all information available before making a decision. Fiduciaries will not be exempt from litigation by merely obtaining a fairness opinion on a proposed transaction, and may be criticized for the real or perceived lack of rigor in the transaction review and analysis.

A recent case involving Disney[13] highlights the risk of failing to perform a rigorous analysis and inspection. The court found that directors who consciously fail to do so may be acting in bad faith or engaging in intentional misconduct, either of which subjects them to personal liability.

3.3.4 A Case for Fiduciary Independence: Howard v. Shay[14]

Background
Pacific Architects & Engineers Inc. was primarily a real estate holding company, with operations in engineering and architecture. In 1972 the company issued an Employee Stock Ownership Plan (ESOP) to benefit current employees.

In 1987 the Pacific Architects & Engineers Inc. board of directors, which included Edward Shay, Martin Lehrer, and Richard Smith, among others, decided to terminate the ESOP through the sale of all outstanding shares. Shay, Lehrer, and Smith were on the board of directors and fiduciaries for the ESOP.

Smith began to search for a firm to perform a valuation analysis of the ESOP stock in order to determine an appropriate selling price. He selected Arthur Young to issue a valuation report and fairness opinion. In July 1988, Shay, a fiduciary of the ESOP, decided to buy the ESOP stock from Pacific Architects & Engineers Inc. Arthur Young determined that $14.40 was an appropriate price to sell the shares. After receiving the valuation report, the Pacific Architects & Engineers Inc. board of directors decided to terminate the ESOP and subsequently voted to sell all shares of ESOP stock to Shay for $14.40 a share. Smith and Shay abstained from voting. Afterward, Lehrer admitted that the special committee decided to sell the ESOP stock to Shay at whatever price Arthur Young recommended, before having seen a valuation report.

The fiduciaries relied exclusively on Arthur Young's valuation; however, upon close inspection it became apparent that there were many flaws or questionable assumptions in Arthur Young's analysis. Arthur Young used a minority and liquidity discount when valuing the shares. Both discounts were well over the normal average used when valuing ESOP stock. Arthur Young also used an additional discount of 60 percent to account for the volatility of Japanese real estate, which would affect a portion of the ESOP stock. Despite these sizable discounts, Arthur Young gave little supporting documentation or data explaining why such excessive discount rates were employed. Total Net Assets implied a share price of $83 per share at the time of the transaction; however, according to Arthur Young's valuation, the shares were only worth $14.40. These assumptions were never questioned by the fiduciaries charged with managing the ESOP.

Following the sale of the ESOP stock, employees of Pacific Architects & Engineers Inc. brought suit against the fiduciaries of the ESOP. The plaintiffs claimed that the fiduciaries' actions showed a " . . . breach of fiduciary duty under the Employee Retirement Income Security Act (ERISA) involving the defendants' administration of an employee stock ownership plan." [15]

Litigation Outcome

The primary question before the court was " . . . whether the fiduciary employed the appropriate methods to investigate the merits of the investment and to structure the investment." The court noted that "ERISA explicitly prohibits a fiduciary from engaging in self-dealing transactions." The court went on to say, "A fiduciary who engages in a self-dealing transaction . . . has the burden of proving that he fulfilled his duties of care and loyalty and that the ESOP received adequate consideration . . .[fiduciaries] are obliged at a minimum to engage in an intensive and scrupulous independent investigation." [16]

The court ruled in favor of the plaintiff, noting that merely hiring an independent financial advisor does not relieve the fiduciaries of their responsibilities to fully investigate all available information before a transaction. The ESOP fiduciaries never demanded any explanation for the underlying assumptions behind the valuation, nor did they take sufficient time to analyze Arthur Young's final report. The court found this to be a breach of their fiduciary responsibility.

Lesson Learned

Hiring an independent financial advisor does not relieve the fiduciaries of their responsibilities to investigate all available information before a transaction. Fiduciaries are required to read, understand, and challenge the methods, assumptions, and conclusions supporting the opinion of an independent financial advisor before relying on such opinion.

3.3.5 A Case for Advisor Independence: Smith v. Shell Petroleum, Inc.[17]

Background

In 1982, Royal Dutch owned nearly 70 percent of Shell Oil Company. Royal Dutch also wholly owned SPNV Holdings, Inc. ("Holdings"), which it created to obtain the remaining outstanding shares of Shell Oil stock held by minority shareholders. In early 1982, Royal Dutch first considered acquiring the minority shares of Shell Oil through either a cash-out merger or a tender offer. Morgan Stanley was retained to establish the value of the minority shares of Shell Oil. However, no action was taken by Holdings at this time.

In 1984, Royal Dutch retained Morgan Stanley to update their analysis of the minority shares of Shell Oil. Morgan Stanley, solely utilizing publicly available information and having no access to probable oil reserves later estimated at over $1 billion, opined that a value of $53 per share was fair. Morgan Stanley was paid a flat fee of $500,000 plus an additional fee of $3.5 million contingent upon deal consummation. This fee structure was not fully disclosed to minority shareholders. Subsequently, Royal Dutch, through Holdings, attempted to merger Shell Oil into Holdings through the offer of $53 per share to all minority shareholders.

The Shell board of directors created a special committee composed of six board members and retained the services of Goldman Sachs to evaluate the Holdings merger offer. Goldman Sachs established that the value range for the minority shares was between $80 and $85 per share. Based on this range, the Shell board of directors decided to reject Holdings' offer and stated that a price of $75 per share was more acceptable.

On March 29, 1984, Royal Dutch abandoned their merger offer and elected to make a tender offer to minority shareholders for $58 per share, despite Goldman Sachs' valuation at over $80 per share and another valuation performed by Donaldson, Lufkin & Jenrette estimating the value of the minority shares at $110 per share.

Holdings, which now owned 93 percent of Shell, was in a unique position at this point due to their fiduciary responsibility to both the majority shareholders attempting to purchase the minority shares and the minority shareholders.

Several shareholders who eventually accepted the tender offer brought a class action suit against Holdings, which was the fiduciary to the minority shares. The minority shareholders argued that Holdings' board failed to meet their fiduciary responsibilities by not fully disclosing all information and by relying on the fairness opinion of Morgan Stanley, which had a conflict of interest, due to the fee structure established by Holdings.

Litigation Outcome

In regards to the bias in Morgan Stanley's valuation, the court stated "although Morgan Stanley's favoritism to Holdings might be assumed from the totality of the circumstances, there are no facts in the record clearly showing that Morgan Stanley deliberately skewed its analysis of Shell's value to attain the result requested by Holdings."

Despite this ruling in favor of the defendants, the court criticized Holdings for not obtaining an independent advisor to assess the fairness of the deal, and for the inherent conflict created as a result of the fee structure. The court stated "the existence of the obvious conflict of interest certainly tends to diminish the validity of Morgan Stanley's opinions."

Lesson Learned

The financial advisor issuing a fairness opinion should be disinterested in the outcome of the board's deliberation on the transaction.

In summary, it is important for the fiduciary to ensure that the transaction review is supported by a well-executed analysis performed by an independent financial advisor, and that the process is free of self-dealing by members of the fiduciary body.

NOTES

1. *Kahn v. Tremont Corp.*, C.A. No. 12339, 1994 WL 162613, at *3 (Del. Ch. Apr. 21, 1994). More recent Delaware court guidance on Independent Committees can be found in *Emerald Partners v. Berlin*, 787 A.2d 85 (Del. Ch. 2003). In addition, *In Re Pure Resources Inc.*, 808 A.2d 421 (Del. Ch. 2002) describes the "free rein and adequate time" an Independent Committee should be afforded.

2. *In Re Fort Howard Corp. Shareholders Litigation*, C.A. No. 9991, 1988 WL 83147, at *12 (Del. Ch. Aug. 8, 1988).

3. Stephen Viederman, "New Directors in Fiduciary Responsibility," *The Global Academy*, October 31, 1985.

4. "Eliot's Fair Play," *New York Post*, May 30, 2003, 41.

5. "NASD Scrutinizes Conflicts in Bankers' Fairness Opinions," *Wall Street Journal*, June 11, 2004, 1.

6. "Fairness Opinions Come to the Fore," *Mergers & Acquisitions: The Dealmakers Journal*, 37.5, May 2002: 16.

7. *Great Western Producers Co-op v. Great Western United Corp.*, 200 Colo. 180, 613 P.2d 873 (1980).

8. *M&F Worldwide v. Perelman*, 799 A.2d 1164 (Del. Ch. 2002).

9. Ibid.

10. *Smith v. Van Gorkom (Trans Union)*, 488 A.2d 858 (Del. Ch. 1985).

11. *Hanson Trust PLC v. ML SCM Acquisition*, 781 F.2d 264 (2d Cir. 1986).

12. *Hanson Trust PLC v. ML SCM Acquisition*, 781 F.2d 264 (2d Cir 1996), quoting *Auerbach v. Bennett*, 47 N.Y.2d 619, 629 (1979).

13. *In Re The Walt Disney Company Derivative Litigation*, 825 A.2d 275 (Del. Ch. 2003).

14. *Howard v. Shay*, 100 F.3d 1484 (9th Cir. 1996).

15. Ibid.

16. Ibid.

17. *Smith v. Shell Petroleum, Inc.*, Civil Action No. 8395, Fed. Sec. L. Rep. P95, 316 (Del. Ch. 1990).

CHAPTER 4

Valuation Methods Employed by Independent Financial Advisors

4.1 INTRODUCTION

The discussion within Section 2.1 introduced some of the conceptual differences between a valuation and a fairness opinion. Despite these differences, some of the analytical tools employed in the valuation exercise are also found in the analysis supporting the fairness opinion. This chapter looks at the basic aspects of the valuation process.

4.1.1 Standard of Value

In framing and undertaking the relevant transaction analytics, one of the first steps for the independent financial advisor is to develop a view regarding the standard of value that will prevail over the analysis. The standard of value is important to both the fairness opinion provider and the fiduciary since it dictates the way in which the supporting analysis is conducted. Using experience and judgment, the financial advisor communicates to the fiduciary the premise or the conceptual framework used. While the independent financial advisor will recommend the appropriate standard of value to employ, ultimately the appropriate standard of value is a legal question. The advisor should clearly articulate the reasons for, and risks associated with, the selection of the standard of value. If the fiduciary has any concerns regarding the standard of value employed, they should be addressed early in the process. Legal counsel should be consulted as well in deciding the standard to be applied.[1]

In valuation theory, there are several defined standards of value. The table below provides some commonly referenced standards of value and their generally accepted meanings.

Standard of Value	Generally Accepted Meaning
Fair Market Value (FMV)	Fair market value is defined by the American Society of Appraisers as "the amount at which property would change hands between a willing seller and a willing buyer when neither is acting under compulsion and when both have reasonable knowledge of the relevant facts."[2]
	The fair market value standard is based on a hypothetical willing buyer and willing seller at arm's length, rather than any particular buyer or seller, as is the case in a fairness opinion analysis. While the hypothetical willing seller is just that, hypothetical, he is motivated to maximize value and will look to sell to a hypothetical buyer in the pool of likely willing buyers.
Fair Value	Fair value is used in a variety of contexts. Fair value under financial reporting standards is defined as the amount at which an asset (or liability) could be bought (or incurred) or sold (or settled) in a current transaction between willing parties, that is, other than in a forced or liquidation sale.[3] Fair value is also a judicially determined standard based on statutes and other legal precedents.
Fundamental Value (often interchangeable with Intrinsic Value)	Fundamental value represents a valuer's judgment regarding an interest's characteristics and how the market would generally assign value to those attributes. The motivations of a particular party, say a controlling shareholder, do not influence the value analysis. Views regarding the highest and best use of the assets are typically not accommodated under this definition. In a fairness opinion analysis, the independent financial advisor will often start with fundamental value, but will then move to consider other standards pertinent to the transaction.
Investment Value	In contrast to fundamental value, investment value does account for the motivations of a particular party. Views regarding the highest and best use of the assets can be accommodated under this definition, under which investment value may include an assessment of investor-specific synergies and tax strategies.
Liquidation Value	There are two valuation approaches within the category of liquidation value often employed for businesses whose ongoing viability is questionable or for businesses that possess significant nonoperating assets: orderly liquidation value, and forced liquidation value (fire sale). Such valuation approaches generally yield a floor value.

The following definitions are also useful to the valuation discussion.

Term	Generally Accepted Meaning
Business Enterprise Value (BEV); often interchanged with Total Invested Capital (TIC) and Market Value of Invested Capital (MVIC)	Value of the entity based on its earning power; often measured as the aggregate market values of all capital (i.e., interest bearing debt plus preferred equity plus common equity)—see chart below.
Price	Current trading price of listed securities.
Market Value of Equity (often interchanged with Market Capitalization or Market Cap)	Current trading price multiplied by current weighted average shares outstanding.
EBIT	Earnings before interest expense and taxes.
EBITDA	Earnings before interest expense, taxes, depreciation, and amortization.
Debt-Free Cash Flows (also referred to as unlevered cash flows)	Valuation terminology to indicate that an earnings or cash flow parameter is calculated before the deduction of interest expense and debt servicing. Converting debt-free cash flows to their present value using the appropriate weighted average return on capital (weighted average cost of capital) yields indications of BEV.
Equity Cash Flows (also referred to as levered cash flows)	Converting equity cash flows (after the deduction of interest expense and debt servicing) to their present value using the return on equity capital (cost of equity) yields indications of Market Value of Equity.
Debt-Free Working Capital	Current assets less current liabilities excluding short-term debt capital component.
Book Value of Equity (also known as Shareholders' Equity)	Accounting term for excess of total assets at historical cost over liabilities, as obtained from the subject company's balance sheet.
Tangible Book Value of Equity	Accounting term for excess of tangible operating assets (e.g., plant, property and equipment, net working capital) at historical cost over liabilities, as obtained from the subject company's balance sheet.
Weighted Average Return on Capital Invested (or Cost of Capital, WACC) (often referred to as the discount rate)	The WACC is an overall rate based upon the expected individual rates of return for total invested capital, i.e., equity and interest-bearing debt.
Return on (Cost of) Equity Capital	The cost of equity in an estimate of return required by equity investors.
Discount Rate	The rate used to discount or convert future cash flows to present value. The discount rate is the WACC for discounting debt-free cash flows or the cost of equity for discounting equity cash flows.

FIGURE 4-1

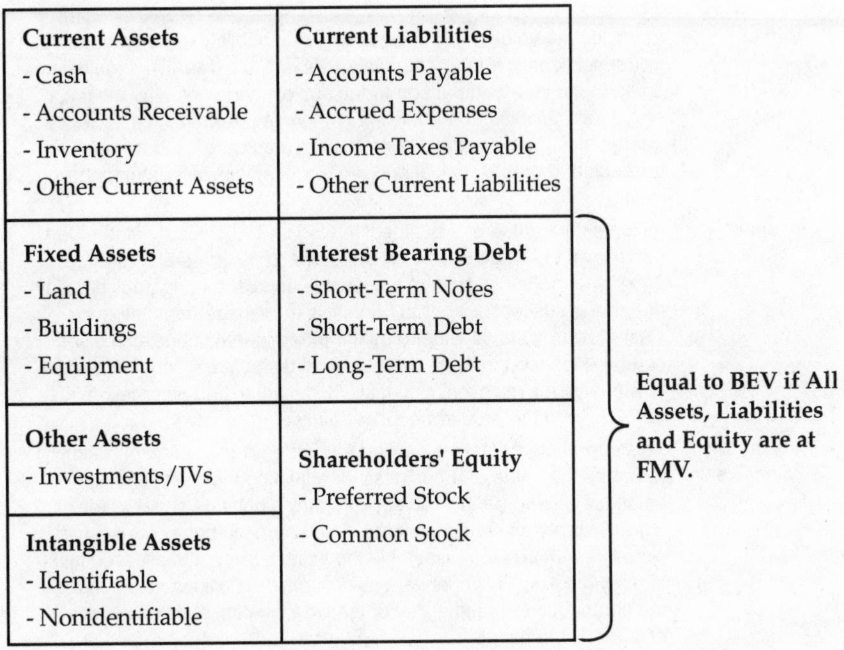

Current Assets - Cash - Accounts Receivable - Inventory - Other Current Assets	Current Liabilities - Accounts Payable - Accrued Expenses - Income Taxes Payable - Other Current Liabilities
Fixed Assets - Land - Buildings - Equipment	Interest Bearing Debt - Short-Term Notes - Short-Term Debt - Long-Term Debt
Other Assets - Investments/JVs	Shareholders' Equity - Preferred Stock - Common Stock
Intangible Assets - Identifiable - Nonidentifiable	

Equal to BEV if All Assets, Liabilities and Equity are at FMV.

The BEV calculation from the FMV balance sheet is illustrated in Figure 4–1.

4.1.2 Approach to Value

Multiple approaches to valuation are utilized. The approaches may produce similar or diverging values. The judgment of the independent financial advisor reconciles the results to achieve an appropriate range for the proposed transaction. This reconciliation process requires quantitative and qualitative judgment, technical expertise, and experienced common sense.

The principal categories of valuation approaches are summarized in the table below. There are a number of variations within each general approach. Many of them were developed to respond to valuation challenges posed by specific factors such as volatility of earnings, asset intensity, intellectual property intensity, balance sheet complexity, and status of the organization in the business lifecycle (e.g., a mature business versus a start-up).

As a practical matter, the independent financial advisor will utilize more than one valuation methodology or approach.

Approach	Overview
Market	Indicates the value of a business by using publicly traded companies or transactions involving companies subject to similar risks (guideline companies) as a comparison to the subject company. The selection of market multiples and guideline companies is qualitative as well as quantitative. Many variations of this approach are used and are applicable to both historical and pro forma prospective operating results.
Income	Indicates the value of a business based on the present value of the cash flows that the business is expected to generate in the future. The courts generally subject the income approach to rigorous scrutiny due to the susceptibility of the analysis to management influence. Cash flow models developed by the independent financial advisor can be enhanced through Real Options techniques, conditional cash flow analysis, simulation, stochastic dominance, and other techniques for managing the problem of uncertainty in cash flows.
Adjusted Balance Sheet	This approach, sometimes called the underlying assets approach, indicates the value of a business by adjusting the asset and liability balances on and off the subject company's balance sheet to their current market value equivalents. This approach considers costs that would be required to reassemble the assets, given an assessed level of utility/functionality under various economic conditions, and considers the contribution to profitability of the working capital, fixed assets, and intangible assets.

4.2 MARKET APPROACH

4.2.1 Overview

In the market determined price of a stock, thousands of investors act through Adam Smith's "invisible hand" to arrive at an equilibrium, or "market" value. [4]

Market-based valuation analysis is based on the premise of the "Law of One Price," [5] where identical assets are deemed to have identical prices. The market-based valuation analysis gauges the value of the subject company or asset by observing prices paid by willing buyers to willing sellers for similar assets. General market data is often viewed as the gold standard for assessing value. When applying market-based valuation methods to value the subject company, one looks to the prices of publicly traded companies subject to similar risks (i.e., guideline companies). This is called the "Guideline Publicly Traded Company" method. The guideline companies may be in the same market as the subject company, may be suppliers, or may

FIGURE 4-2

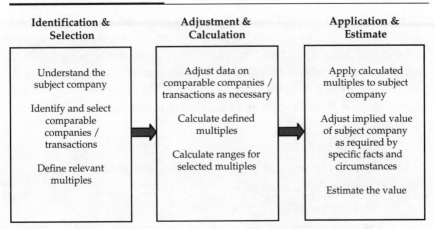

Identification & Selection	Adjustment & Calculation	Application & Estimate
Understand the subject company	Adjust data on comparable companies / transactions as necessary	Apply calculated multiples to subject company
Identify and select comparable companies / transactions	Calculate defined multiples	Adjust implied value of subject company as required by specific facts and circumstances
Define relevant multiples	Calculate ranges for selected multiples	Estimate the value

be customers. The observed market prices are converted to value multiples (e.g., price-to-earnings ratio). The multiples can then be used to derive indicated market values for the subject company or asset. Though not infallible, market data should be collected and analyzed wherever possible.

The market-based valuation analysis is comprised of three general phases, as illustrated in Figure 4–2.

The three main phases consist of the following steps:

1. Identification and selection of transaction targets or publicly traded companies that operate in the same industry or are influenced by the same underlying economics as the subject company. The business and financial profiles are analyzed for similarity to the subject company.

2. Adjustment to normalize the financial results of the comparable companies as appropriate, and calculation of valuation multiples (e.g., Business Enterprise Value to EBITDA).

3. Application of the valuation multiples to the relevant financial results of the subject company, in order to estimate value. Various adjustments are made as necessary for working capital excesses or deficits, nonoperating assets or liabilities, debt, and controlling and/or nonmarketability considerations. The value of the subject company is adjusted to reflect the subject interest in the company.

Further details regarding each of the foregoing steps are provided in the sections below.

4.2.2 Identification and Selection

When selecting publicly traded companies as guideline companies, the underlying economics driving the guideline companies should be similar to those that drive the subject company. Comparable underlying business risk is essential to drawing value inferences from companies deemed to provide guideline multiples to apply to the subject business. Factors that often guide the identification and selection of market analogs for the subject business or asset are:

+ Lines of business
+ Basis of competition (e.g., price, performance, service, style)
+ Target markets, customers
+ Production strategy
+ Business structure (e.g., holding company, diversified business)
+ Industry position (e.g., leader, follower)
+ Investment opportunity set
+ Size (absolute, and relative to competitors in terms of revenues and market capitalization)
+ Geography and diversification
+ Financial condition
+ Other risk and performance characteristics
+ Asset and earnings quality
+ Other performance measures (e.g., margins, returns)

In addition, the independent financial advisor assesses how the market is pricing a guideline company candidate (price discovery). Of particular interest is the way in which the market appears to process information about the guideline companies (and the subject company, if it is publicly traded) and to impact market valuations for good news as well as bad news.

Where there exists data on companies subject to comparable risks and that are engaged in merger and acquisition activity, guideline transaction data should also be used. This is called the "Guideline Merged and Acquired Company" method. Data sources for transaction information are discussed in Section 4.2.5.

After the guideline transactions have been identified and selected, financial and operating valuation multiples are determined. These multiples provide representative benchmarks for the market values of companies in the industry, with attributes similar to those of the subject business. Selection of the multiples to apply to the subject company's relevant parameters is based on judgment, supported by available quantitative and qualitative evidence.

Select examples of valuation multiples are shown in the following table.

Multiples	Relevant Operating Parameter(s)	Magnitude of Multiple Influenced by	Applicable Cases
Business Enterprise Value/Revenue	Revenue	• Economic and industry growth • Market share • Revenue growth • Brand	• Comparable profit margins and growth prospects • Start-up company • Roll-up

Earnings Multiples
For example:
  Business Enterprise Value/EBITDA and
  Business Enterprise Value/EBIT
  Equity
  Price/Earnings
	Earnings before interest expense, taxes, depreciation, and amortization (EBITDA)
	Earnings before interest and taxes (EBIT)
	Net Income
		• Growth in margins and overall profitability	• Mature, going concern
			• Portfolio companies
			• Asset-intensive businesses

Book Value Multiples Price/Book Equity Price/Tangible Equity	Book Value Total Shareholders' Equity Total Shareholders' Equity less Book Value of Intangible Assets	• Return on assets (ROA) • Age of assets • Return on equity (ROE)	• Financial services businesses • Insurance • Holding companies
Operating Multiples	Operating performance metrics, such as number of cable subscribers, acute care beds, retail selling square footage, etc.	• Industry specifics	• Industry convention (cable television, health care, broadcasting, certain retail)

Early stage companies such as technology start-ups or biotech firms pose special valuation challenges (see Section 6.4).

4.2.3 Adjustment and Calculation

The independent financial advisor will make a variety of adjustments to normalize the operating parameters of the guideline companies. Such adjustments are to be expected; in fact, the absence of adjustments in the independent financial advisor's analysis should be more alarming than their presence. Once the adjustments have been made, the market valuation multiples can be calculated.

Observed multiples for the comparable companies may reflect the influence of nonrecurring charges and different accounting policies:

♦ Extraordinary or nonrecurring items, such as merger and acquisition expenses and restructuring charges, must be removed from the income statement.

♦ Accounting basis needs to be comparable (e.g., inventory needs to be presented on either LIFO or FIFO basis; consistent depreciation method and lives should be used for fixed assets).

♦ Nonoperating items or excess assets need to be excluded.

♦ Discontinued operations must be removed from historical financial statements.

In forming a view of concluded ranges for selected multiples, the independent financial advisor will consider guideline company and subject company characteristics such as:

♦ Greater growth opportunities generally result in higher multiples.

♦ Recent poor performance may result in higher multiples, if problems are expected to be temporary.

♦ Strong market positioning (and growth rates) may result in higher multiples.

♦ Multiples are often positively correlated with projected growth and strong relative return performance (ROE).

♦ Multiples for small "players" in an industry are generally lower than for large "players," reflecting risk differences.

Some common pitfalls in using valuation multiples include:

♦ Failure to conduct an adequate search for comparable company data.

♦ Failure to make appropriate financial statement adjustments to comparable companies.

♦ If the numerator represents business enterprise value (debt plus equity capital), the denominator should reflect income that is available to both debt and equity holders (i.e., revenue or earnings before interest expense is deducted). Price or equity in the numerator would require a denominator that reflects the residual income available to equity holders (i.e., net income).

♦ Reliance on an EBITDA multiple as the sole market valuation indicator.

♦ Simple reliance on average of so-called comparable company multiples without thorough analysis to determine if they truly serve as guideline companies to the subject company.

♦ Potential issues with using public market and transaction data. These issues are discussed below.

Sole use of EBITDA multiples as a value indicator has at times led to incorrect value conclusions. EBITDA ignores the needed investments in net working capital during periods of growth. Even in industries that are not viewed as capital intensive, increases in working capital investment are real uses of cash flows. EBITDA also fails to consider the cash requirements due to the amount of required investment for replacement of assets in industries with generally short-lived assets and investments needed to meet revenue forecasts.

4.2.4 Apply and Estimate

Following the calculation of adjusted multiples, indications of the subject company's value can be calculated by applying selected multiples to the relevant financial result of the subject company. Best practice is to conclude on a range from the valuation multiples. Once this range is established, the independent financial advisor will form an opinion regarding the relative comfort achieved when comparing the proposed transaction pricing to the reference range for the subject business or assets. The independent financial advisor will often illustrate his or her findings under this approach as shown in Figure 4–3.

4.2.5 Merger and Acquisition Data

Information gleaned from merger and acquisition pricing can be used to indicate the value of private companies and divisions of public companies. Multiples of value can be derived from transaction data by analyzing a

FIGURE   4-3

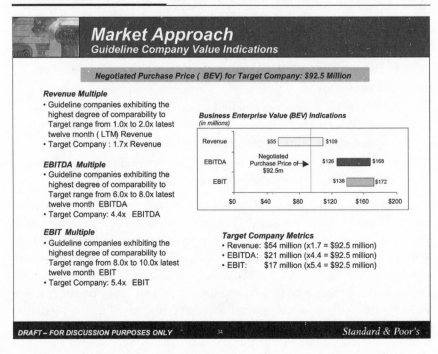

Market Approach
Guideline Company Value Indications

Negotiated Purchase Price (BEV) for Target Company: $92.5 Million

Revenue Multiple
• Guideline companies exhibiting the highest degree of comparability to Target range from 1.0x to 2.0x latest twelve month (LTM) Revenue
• Target Company : 1.7x Revenue

EBITDA Multiple
• Guideline companies exhibiting the highest degree of comparability to Target range from 6.0x to 8.0x latest twelve month EBITDA
• Target Company: 4.4x EBITDA

EBIT Multiple
• Guideline companies exhibiting the highest degree of comparability to Target range from 8.0x to 10.0x latest twelve month EBIT
• Target Company: 5.4x EBIT

Business Enterprise Value (BEV) Indications
(in millions)

Revenue — $55 — $109
EBITDA — Negotiated Purchase Price of $92.5m — $126 — $168
EBIT — $138 — $172

$0 $40 $80 $120 $160 $200

Target Company Metrics
• Revenue: $54 million (x1.7 = $92.5 million)
• EBITDA: $21 million (x4.4 = $92.5 million)
• EBIT: $17 million (x5.4 = $92.5 million)

DRAFT – FOR DISCUSSION PURPOSES ONLY   34   Standard & Poor's

target company's purchase price relative to its historical financial and operating performance.

When determining the guideline transactions to use in developing the transaction multiples, the independent financial advisor considers the following:

♦ How comparable is the target company in the transaction to the subject business in the case at hand in terms of industry, perform-ance (margins, leverage), size (total capitalization, sales, assets), etc.? The less comparable the target business, the less instructive the transaction.

♦ Is the target company in the transaction private or public? Less information is typically available for private companies.

♦ How close is the reference transaction date to the subject transac-tion's date? The further apart the two dates are, the less instructive the reference transaction may be.

♦ How reliable are the sources of data? Is it possible to verify the data available (consideration paid/received, transaction date, financial statement data) with a reliable source such as an 8-K (U.S. corporate filing if the transaction was material to the acquirer)? It is not uncommon for various news sources to report differing multiples.

♦ If more than one source (*Securities Data, Bloomberg, Mergerstat,* etc.) is available, are the facts and data consistent? When there are no reliable sources available and the data is inconsistent among sources, the reference transaction may be rendered useless.

♦ Is the reported purchase price for an equity interest or for the entire entity (i.e., equity plus debt assumed)?

♦ What percent of the target is being acquired, and does it represent a controlling or a minority interest? Often, a seemingly minority purchase will allow the acquirer effective control of the company due to previous acquisitions or affiliated ownership.

♦ Control contests can squeeze prices. Observed transactions might temporarily reflect scavenging for marginal votes in a control contest, or an effort to assemble an influential block. Conversely, sometimes the only shares traded are loose minority shares that will get abused in the aftermath of a larger control contest. If this were the case, it would not be appropriate to take such prices as guideline for the value of the target company.

When calculating transaction multiples, the market value of the equity component typically represents a controlling interest, but may be less than 100 percent ownership. Therefore, the market value of equity needs to be adjusted (or grossed up) to a value that reflects 100 percent of the company for the purpose of deriving applicable valuation multiples.

4.3 INCOME APPROACH (OR DISCOUNTED CASH FLOW METHOD)

4.3.1 Overview

The discounted cash flow (DCF) method is a frequently used variation of the income approach to valuation. A DCF analysis is based on the present value of expected (risk-adjusted) cash flow projections for the subject business or asset. A stream of future earnings, cash flows, or asset values is projected, and then converted to present value using an appropriate opportunity rate of return oftentimes called a cost of capital.

The concept underlying a DCF analysis is that the realistic valuation of any business or asset is directly related to the future cash flow generation

FIGURE 4-4

attributable to such business or asset. Future cash flow represents the recovery of investment as well as a return on investment. Under this premise, the ability of a business enterprise to create adequate cash flow, fund required cash disbursements, reinvest in the assets (tangible and intangible) required to support anticipated levels of operation, and provide for related financing activities is the primary determinant of value in that enterprise. A key challenge for the independent financial advisor is to ensure that the approach to quantifying cash flows is clearly articulated, and also that the cash flows used are adequately defined.

This valuation technique also identifies and highlights specific "value drivers" that support the cash flow projections, such as the price and volume characteristics inherent in projected revenue/sales, the fixed and variable costs required to produce the projected revenues, the working capital and capital expenditure investments likely needed to support the project level of operations, and other factors that directly impact the prospective cash flow generating ability and current value of the subject business or asset.

The DCF analysis for either debt-free or equity cash flows generally consists of the steps and considerations shown in Figure 4–4.

4.3.2 Identify and Analyze the Appropriate Projections of Cash Flows

A major requirement of the discounted cash flow approach is a cash flow forecast. This forecast typically reflects management's best estimate of what will most likely occur in the future as it pertains to revenues, expenses, capital expenditure, and working capital requirements. The independent financial advisor will consider and employ, where appropriate, any existing financial projections provided by management. During the valuation analysis, the forecast is evaluated by comparison to the historical and forecasted financial and operating results of guideline businesses, with an emphasis on growth and profitability. See Chapter 5 for a fuller discussion on cash flow projections.

The business model should reflect a period when the business is reaching a state with constant growth into perpetuity before the terminal value can be calculated. This is the "normalized" business. "Normalized" residual annual free cash flow should reflect the following considerations:

♦ Sales growth from the last projection period by the assumed residual growth rate.

♦ Operating margins are set at "normal" levels.

♦ Capital expenditures should be adequate to sustain growth.

♦ Net working capital investment should be adequate to support sales growth.

♦ Depreciation must have a sustainable relation with capital expenditure.

For purposes of this overview of the DCF analysis, the cash flow calculation can be illustrated as follows:

> Revenue
> − Operating Expenses (Excluding Interest Expense)
> ───
> Earnings Before Interest Expense and Taxes (EBIT)
>
> − Cash Income Taxes
> ─────────────────────
>
> = Debt-Free Net Income (Before Deduction of Interest Expense)
>
> + Depreciation, Amortization, and Deferred Charges
> −/+ Change (increase/decrease) in Net Working Capital
> − Capital Expenditures
> ─────────────────────────
>
> = Debt-Free Cash Flow (Reflects Cash Flow Available to Service and Provide a Return to Debt and Equity Investors)

4.3.3 Compute the Terminal Value

Terminal value, also known as "residual value," represents the value of the cash flows occurring *after* the discrete projection period. Most businesses are assumed to have an indefinite life beyond the period modeled. Two primary conventions have been developed for the quantification of this terminal (end of discrete projection period) or residual value analysis.

One approach is to calculate terminal value by capitalizing the normalized residual annual cash flow deemed supportable at the end of the projection period. It can be seen in the formula:

$$\text{Terminal Value} = \frac{\text{Normalized Debt-Free Cash Flow}}{(\text{WACC minus Long-Term Expected Average Growth in Cash Flows})}$$

An alternative to this approach is to utilize prevailing M&A based valuation multiple evidence in the industry sector to derive value indications for the subject business based upon normalized earnings or other operating parameters at the end of the discrete projection period. Use of M&A multiples are fraught with the problems inherent in using any industry multiple, as discussed above in Section 4.2. Any such multiple must reflect the expected cash flow growth rate inherent in the business at the end of the discrete projection period, not the growth rate as of today's valuation date.

What is the appropriate denominator in the terminal value calculation?

+ The discount rate must reflect the risk of the cash flows in the numerator.
+ Long-term average growth rate estimates should be checked for reasonableness by comparing to hard benchmarks:
  + Nominal GDP growth
  + Projected nominal growth for the industry
  + The risk-free rate
+ The growth rate g may be negative (perpetual shrinkage).

4.3.4 Discount Projected Cash Flows and Terminal Value by Appropriate Rate of Return

The projected cash flows and terminal value are converted to their present value equivalent by discounting at the discount rate. The discount rate is the rate of return that reflects the time value of money adjusted for the risk of an investment in the capital of the subject company.

The discount rate is an overall rate based upon the expected individual rates of return for invested capital, i.e., equity and interest-bearing debt. This rate, commonly called the weighted average cost of capital, or WACC, is calculated by weighting the required returns on long-term interest-bearing debt capital and common equity capital in proportion to their estimated percentages in an assumed optimal capital structure.

The discount rate should be matched with the nature of the projected cash flows. If the cash flows to be discounted are expressed in "real" terms—i.e., adjusted to remove the effects of inflation—then a "real" discount rate should be used. If cash flows are projected in "nominal" terms—i.e., incorporating inflationary growth—then a "nominal" discount rate should be used. The handling of income tax issues when calculating a textbook WACC, such as the likely deductability of interest expense in the year incurred, is simplistic. The textbook WACC requires very restrictive assumptions that may not be realistic.

WACC may be impacted by factors such as specific assumptions about:

♦ High leverage
♦ Complex tax situations
♦ Complex capital structures
♦ Unusual ownership structures
♦ Exotic securities
♦ Dynamic rather than static situations

The rate used to discount projected cash flows of the subject company may be adjusted for factors such as:

♦ Risk in the capital structure
♦ Currency risk
♦ Certain investor characteristics
♦ A firm's size and risk profile
♦ Risk in realizing future tax deductions generated by interest expense

Good practice in the area of cost of capital suggests, however, that wherever possible, company-specific risks should be addressed within the derivation of cash flows, as opposed to through the use of highly subjective adjustments to the discount rate employed.

The discount rate should not be confused with the "cost of funds" used for comparing alternative funding sources. It should also not be confused with the "hurdle rate" used to evaluate projects in the capital budgeting process of the company. It is also not a prevailing interest rate or other indicator of capital market or macroeconomic conditions.

The table below provides a glossary of terms and definitions typically associated with the cost of capital discussion.

Term	Definition	Method of Calculation	Inputs/Sources
Weighted average cost of capital (WACC)	Rate of return that reflects the risk of an investment in the capital of the company (debt and equity), as well as the time value of money.	Weighted required returns on interest-bearing debt and equity in proportion to their estimated percentages in capital structure.	Calculated company's cost of equity and cost of debt, as well as assumed optimal or actual expected industry capital structure.
Cost of equity	Rate of return that reflects the future risk of an investment in company's equity, as well as the time value of money.	Required return is measured by relative risk.	Risk-free rate (U.S. Treasury rate), risk adjusted equity premium.
Cost of debt	Rate of return a prudent debt investor would require today on interest-bearing debt.	Since the interest expense on debt capital employed is deductible for income tax purposes, an interest rate adjusted for the tax deductability of interest is used.	Corporate debt yield of appropriate grade, depending on financial condition of the subject company, risks of its operations, and the assumed capital structure.
Cost of preferred stock	Rate of return a prudent debt investor would require today on preferred stock.	Because of certain provisions in the U.S. tax code, investors may accept a yield that is actually lower than that of compara-ble corporate bonds. Since dividends on preferred equity are not deductible for income tax purposes, no adjustment for corporate income taxes is necessary.	Often, preferred stock is priced similarly to corporate debt. Preferred stock may have special redemption or conversion options that may impact the value (and required return).
Internal rate of return (IRR)	The rate of return generated by an investment in a project.	Discount rate that makes the net present value of investment and future cash flows equal to zero.	Calculated based on project cash flows and initial investment.

Term	Definition	Method of Calculation	Inputs/Sources
Hurdle rate	Minimum rate of return required for positive internal project in a capital budgeting process.	Generally set by company management.	Often set at cost of capital "plus" subjective amount to account for optimistic cash flow projections in capital budget proposals, and a sufficient amount to earn on income-producing projects to cover the cost of mandated expenditures (e.g., OSHA, environmental, etc.).

A more extensive discussion of WACC and discount rates can be found in Appendix V.

4.3.5 Compute Business Enterprise Value and Adjust for Nonoperating Assets and Liabilities

BEV is computed as the sum of the present value of the projected cash flows and the terminal value as of the valuation date. The value of any noncore assets (e.g., excess investments or working capital) should be added to the BEV. The values of noncore liabilities (e.g., environmental cleanup on shutdown plant, or shortage of working capital) are then subtracted. The net result represents a value indication for the subject enterprise.

4.3.6 Allocate Business Enterprise Value to Subject Interest Taking into Account Adjustments for Liquidity and Control Characteristics

Once a value indication for the subject company has been determined, the focus of the analysis shifts to the specific nature and characteristics of the subject interest and the facts and circumstances surrounding the proposed transaction. Where the entire enterprise interest is not the subject of the fairness opinion, the total value is apportioned to the interest subject to the opinion. Appropriate discount(s) and/or premia applicable to the specific interest are then applied.

FIGURE 4-5

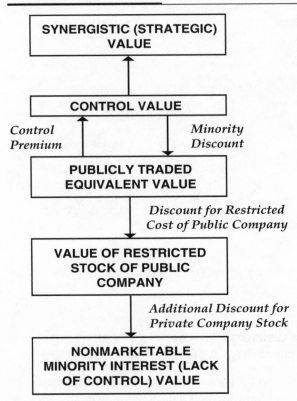

The chart in Figure 4–5 summarizes potential premia or discounts to an interest's value that may be appropriate.

See Chapter 7, Section 7.2 for a more detailed discussion of discounts and premia.

After the interest's value has been adjusted for any applicable discount or premium, a value indication under the income approach has been determined. A range of values is appropriate for the fairness opinion analysis because of the potential difference in assumptions and risks.

4.4 ADJUSTED BALANCE SHEET APPROACH

The adjusted balance sheet approach recognizes that a prudent investor would not ordinarily pay more for the assemblage of assets than the sum of the values of the underlying tangible and intangible assets minus the liabilities assumed. This approach is sometimes called the underlying assets approach.

Valuers employ one or more approaches when valuing the underlying assets of a business. The approaches can be categorized into three broad categories: the market approach, the income approach, and the cost approach.

The general theory of the market approach to valuing underlying assets parallels the discussion of the guideline transactions approach above. The transactions one considers are based on the similarity in utility of the acquired asset to that of the subject assets.

The market approach is commonly used when valuing the following underlying assets/liabilities:

- Common and preferred shares of publicly traded companies held as investments
- Option contracts and other derivatives
- Real estate
- Majority/minority-owned closely held subsidiaries or operating companies
- Certain intangible assets (i.e., patents, trademarks, franchise rights)
- Public debt (corporate bonds) outstanding

The general theory of the income approach to valuing underlying assets parallels the discussion of the income approach above. The income or cash flow attributable to a specific asset must be measured. This measurement process often entails allocating returns to contributory assets to isolate the cash flow attributable to the subject asset (i.e., assets that are needed along with the subject asset in order for the owner of the subject asset to generate a return). At a minimum, contributory assets are working capital investments and fixed asset investments needed to produce the products developed with the intellectual capital of the subject company.

The income approach is commonly used when valuing the following underlying assets:

- Thinly traded shares of public companies held for investment
- Real estate
- Majority/minority-owned closely held subsidiaries or operating companies
- Certain intangible assets (i.e., patents, trademarks, franchise rights)
- Debt (mortgages, term debt)

The general theory of the cost approach to valuing underlying assets is that an investor would not normally pay more for an asset than the cost to replace it with an asset of equal utility. Typically, the first step in the cost approach is to estimate "replacement cost new" of an asset, using current materials, prices, and labor. "Replacement cost" is considered to be the cost of substituting an asset with another asset having the equivalent functional utility as the asset being appraised.

If reproduction cost, instead of replacement cost, is used as a beginning point, then an adjustment must be made to take into account the excess costs that may be represented in reproduction cost compared to replacement cost. "Reproduction cost" is the estimated cost to construct, at current prices, an exact duplicate, or replica, of the asset being appraised, using the same materials, construction standards, design, layout, and quality of workmanship, and embodying all the subject's deficiencies, superadequacies, and obsolescence.

The estimated replacement cost new should include "turn-key" costs needed to get the asset up and running, and a "developer's" profit for the risks the sellers took in assembling the asset and getting into a productive state. The replacement cost new is then reduced by the amount of depreciation, resulting from physical deterioration, functional obsolescence, and economic/external obsolescence, that is inherent in the asset—in other words, how much less utility will be provided by the subject asset compared to the new asset? The resulting depreciated replacement cost is an indication of value for the asset. The factors of depreciation are:

> *Physical Depreciation* as a result of age and wear can be divided into curable and incurable. Curable physical deterioration is a loss in value that can be recovered or offset by repairing or replacing defective items causing the loss—provided that the resulting value increase equals or exceeds the cost of work. Incurable physical deterioration, on the other hand, is a loss in value that cannot be offset or whose correction would involve a cost greater than the resulting increase in value and be thought of as "loss of service life"—that is, how long would the new asset provide the investor with utility versus the subject asset? Physical depreciation is not a factor in the valuation of intangible assets.
>
> *Functional Obsolescence* is any loss in value resulting from inappropriate design, inefficient process flow, poor construction or layout for the intended use, or changes in the state-of-the-art. Functional obsolescence, which can be measured in terms of excess operating costs for either tangible or intangible assets, may be either curable or incurable.
>
> *Economic/External Obsolescence* relates to the loss in value that occurs from factors external to the assets, i.e., when the operating profits of a business

do not support the underlying asset value of the business under the "value in continued use" premise. In other words, the investor cannot earn a fair return on the estimated value before economic/external obsolescence because output prices are too low or input prices are too high, capacity is too great given demand for the output, etc.

The cost approach is commonly used when valuing the following underlying assets:

♦ Machinery and equipment

♦ Buildings and site improvements

♦ Some intangible assets (e.g., in-house software, by calculating the cost to replicate the software)

Some independent financial advisors have fully credentialed tangible asset (e.g., real estate, plant, property and equipment) valuation practitioners. These individuals may be MAI certified real estate valuation professionals, engineers, and others with expertise in the machinery and equipment market.

The cost approach is often used by independent financial advisors to corroborate asset value indications derived using other methodologies, like income and market approaches. Cost approach to internal projects may also become the basis for buy versus build decisions.

The adjusted balance sheet approach of valuing the BEV is applicable where the going concern status of the target is in question. Under the premise of potential liquidation, there are two variations of the above approaches that may be used: orderly liquidation value and forced liquidation value (fire sale). Such valuation approaches generally yield a floor value.

NOTES

1. See *Kahn v. Household Acquisition Corp.*, (Del Ch. May 6, 1998) (1988 Del Ch. LEXIS 64, at *32-34). Jay W. Eisenhofer and John L. Reed, "Valuation Litigation," *Delaware Journal of Corporate Law*, vol. 22, 1997, 112-26.

2. American Society of Appraisers, Business Valuation Standards—Definitions.

3. Statement of Financial Accounting Standards No. 141, Business Combinations.

4. Kent Hickman and Glenn H. Petry, "A Comparison of Stock Price Predictions Using Court Accepted Formulas, Dividend Discount and P/E Models," *Financial Management*, Summer 1999, 84.

5. Law, J. (1997) [1705] "Money and Trade Considered, with a Proposal for Supplying the Nation with Money," in A. E. Murphy (ed), *Monetary Theory 1601-1758*, vol. 5, London: Routledge.

CHAPTER 5

Projections

The need for speed in getting the transaction completed must be balanced with the need for confidence in the business case. The role of the independent financial advisor in issuing a fairness opinion is not to create a new set of projections, but rather, to gain confidence in management's forecasts and assumptions. Ideally, this is done collaboratively with management (and others) through due diligence, interviews with key financial and operating management in the organization, and independent research and information gathering.

This process helps focus attention on risks inherent in the operating projections, and it facilitates explicit modeling of these risks in the cash flows—through scenario analysis, probability adjustment, or other means. The resulting *expected case* cash flows are, or should be, the primary input in the DCF analysis. The expected case cash flows should be a probability-weighted compilation of potential outcomes. Examining the probabilities associated with potential outcomes—as, for instance, likelihoods of 10 percent, 50 percent, and 90 percent—enables the fiduciary and the independent financial advisor to more fully understand the degree of risk associated with realizing the expected case cash flows. Furthermore, examining the assumptions underlying the alternative outcomes can lead to either (a) contingency planning or (b) alterations to the deal framework, terms, or postdeal strategy in order to mitigate potential risks and capitalize on identified upsides.

5.1 WHO SHOULD PREPARE AND REVIEW THE PROJECTIONS?

Management projections will be used as the starting point for the independent financial advisor's analysis. Management will be charged with delivering the business case after the transaction is completed. The fiduciary body may have already been intimately involved in the review and approval of such projections. Ultimately, the independent financial advisor must form its own conclusions regarding forecasts and assumptions, and their relevance to the proposed transaction.

The independent financial advisor will need to understand management's expected case.

One could expect that management may have prepared multiple sets of projections. The interrelationship between the assumptions in these sets of projections needs to be analyzed, as does the sensitivity of the indicated values based on the underlying assumptions. The independent financial advisor will investigate the process by which the projections were assembled. The measurement and reporting functions within the target company are often complex and not completely integrated.

The independent financial advisor cannot provide assurances that the financial picture presented by management is error free. However, it can assess the reasonability of the overall financial and operating views of management through reference to the actual achievements of comparable industry participants and other analytical procedures.

The views of management will be tested against a variety of independently derived data:

- Financial and operating disclosures of publicly traded companies
- Industry and government surveys
- Credit analyst and investment banking reports
- Phone interviews
- Econometric forecasts
- Regulatory publications
- Academic studies
- Independent consultants retained to address specific technical issues
- Other sources

Once the independent financial advisor has conducted due diligence on available forecasts, adjustments are made to reflect independently derived views of assumptions and value drivers. A detailed road map of changes made to the financial forecasts, and the resulting impact on value indications, should be developed. A flexible financial model prepared by the independent financial advisor for valuation purposes will accommodate this process. Scenarios can be run on key value drivers to establish a range of potential outcomes and the probability of realizing the forecasted outcome. Modeling techniques, such as simulation (i.e., probabilistic analysis of alternative outcomes), accommodate this process. Central to the independent financial advisor's activities here is good communication with both management and the fiduciary.

5.2 GOOD HYGIENE IN PROJECTION BUILDING

From a fairness opinion provider's perspective, some of the characteristics of good projections should include the following points.

5.2.1 Input Across the Organization

Does the company utilize an integrated process that incorporates input from all parts of the organization to arrive at consistent and reasonable assumptions? If it takes multiple functions to deliver value to customers and ultimately to the company's shareholders, then it stands to reason that these functions provide input in the projection process. The basic building blocks in each organizational unit (e.g., price and volume, fixed and variable expenses, taxes, working capital requirements, and reinvestment requirements) should be adequately addressed.

5.2.2 Corroboration with External Sources

Management needs to corroborate market size, growth, and share assumptions as well as operating cost assumptions, working capital investment, and capital expenditure requirements with external industry sources. These include third-party providers of market and industry research, analyst expectations, and, in many cases, collaboration with an industry or technical expert. As stated elsewhere, market data is the gold standard in financial analysis. Financial projections should incorporate relevant market-derived information wherever possible.

For example, such data can be particularly useful in natural resource and commodity industries such as oil and natural gas, commodities that have a robust and well-developed futures market. An oil company could provide a set of projections based on future oil price assumptions that were inconsistent with the futures market for oil. Such projections could only be tenable if the oil company possessed specific knowledge about prices not reflected in market prices/futures trading.

5.2.3 Assumptions

Projections may incorporate implicit or undisclosed assumptions. The assumption sets used by management should be transparent. The independent financial advisor must achieve a confidence level with the assumptions, and this can only be accomplished through investigation/Q&A. Dramatic improvements in any key financial metric as compared with historical trends require strong supporting evidence in order to be credible. For example: Why is it credible that the sales staff will be twice as productive next year? Why is it credible that R&D costs will drop after the next product launch, rather than continue? Why is it credible that growth trends will continue?

It is often assumed that the classic "hockey stick" forecast in sales growth is caused by unrealistic assumptions. However, this may not always be the case. Dramatic increases in sales levels relative to historical performance can be plausible and validated by the independent financial advisor if the critical assumptions are transparent and supportable. Developments in products, competitors, and markets can conspire to provide significant growth opportunities. The key is to gain an understanding and confidence from the "bottom up" in the assumptions used to develop the price, volume, profitability, and capital investment assumptions. No assumption in the forecast should be summarily dismissed or left unquestioned.

5.2.4 Systematically Identify and Assess Uncertainty

Good managers seek to identify and quantify uncertainty. Only by embracing uncertainty in this way can effective management planning and decision making occur. Typically, a business case assumes that there is exactly one fixed view of the future. A comprehensive assessment of uncertainty often yields projections that are not symmetric (i.e., more downside impact or upside impact). Business outcomes are not always distributed symmetrically around the expected case. It should be standard operating procedure to deal with ranges of outcomes in sales, costs, and level of reinvestment in the business.

In addition, certain events that could significantly impact the value of a business upward (i.e., new products) or downward (i.e., a catastrophic event such as loss of a major customer) can also be modeled given a reasonable assessment of the economic impact and likelihood of the event. It is highly recommended that business uncertainty be dealt with in the cash flows, as opposed to subjective adjustments in factors such as the discount rate. Uncertainty around value drivers can be addressed using a variety of tools.

5.2.5 Considered Alternatives to the Proposed Transaction

Confidence that the proposed deal terms are fair stems not exclusively from the Net Present Value of the expected cash flows of the business, but rather, from the Net Present Value of the expected cash flows of the "deal world" as compared to the "nondeal world." In order to make this distinction, questions such as the following should be asked: What would *really* happen in the "no deal" scenario? What's *really* the next best alternative? Does management have a "road map" that outlines the different courses of action the company may take, given different outcomes?

For example, if a business is being divested, the value to the seller is not the stand-alone value of the business being sold, but potentially that value plus any internal synergies being lost due to the divestiture. Alternatively, if a buyer is considering the acquisition of a high risk/high reward business, has management considered that if things go poorly, the business could be shut down? In converse, if things go extremely well, has management considered how line extensions and expansion of the business would increase value in the upside scenario? Failure to consider value-increasing contingent strategies could lead to an undervaluation of the transaction. Such contingent strategies are examples of "real options."

Good managers consider real options in the planning process. Tools such as influence diagrams can help structure alternatives and model probabilistic parameters. It is important to consider all of the contingent strategies that may increase value in assessing a proposed transaction. Failure to do so could lead to an underappreciation of value of the proposed transaction.

5.3 ROLE OF SYNERGIES

5.3.1 What Is Synergy?

Pfizer acquired Pharmacia on April 16, 2003, for $60 billion. Pfizer paid a 28 percent premium over the prevailing share price of Pharmacia. In 2003,

Alcan acquired Pechiney for $6.4 billion, a premium of 55 percent over the target's prevailing share price. Data exists regarding premia paid for public targets in 371 deals across 50 industries in 2003. The average premium paid by buyers was 62.3 percent in 2003. In 1999, the average premium paid was 43.3 percent for the 723 deals observed. [1]

Why would a buyer pay such a premium over a pretransaction price the market perceives to be the value of a target company? *Synergy* is the near universal justification.

Synergy is a concept of two or more things coexisting harmoniously such that the two (or more) working together can produce better outcomes than the sum of what each could produce alone. The underlying tenet is that more value is derived from two businesses operating in concert than each operating independently on their own. The synergistic value arises from being able to do more, which might mean having access to more markets, to the delivery of more products and services, reaching more customers, gaining distribution channels, and having an overall lower unit cost per revenue dollar. To the extent that the perceived value exists solely in the stand-alone entities, there should be no material transaction synergies reflected in the price.

It is the transaction negotiations that determine the sharing, if any, of the synergies. The sharing is reflected in the price premium. See Section 6.3 for more discussion on synergies in transaction pricing.

5.3.2 Synergy in the Fairness Analysis

The purchase price to be paid in a transaction may reflect or include the anticipated benefits or perceived benefits/value of synergies. The challenge for the fairness opinion provider is to understand the basis for the synergy, how it will be realized, over what time period, and its corresponding value. Moreover, it is incumbent upon the fairness opinion provider to communicate to the fiduciary body the role of synergies in the analysis so that the fiduciary body is equipped to assess the risk of the pricing analysis relative to its own view of the achievability and value of the identified synergies.

Synergistic issues tend to exist in the buyer's analysis. Therefore, it is important that the analysis from the buyer's perspective address the risks of synergy realization. In contrast, synergies appear less often on the seller's side because entities being divested usually either have low synergies with any parent organization or the deal is structured in such a way that those synergistic effects on other divisions are maintained in the postdeal world.

The value indications developed by the independent financial advisor will first consider those revenue and operating cost initiatives that are achievable without the transaction. Synergies will be modeled under various scenarios to quantify the value implications to the post-transaction entity. Sharing synergy values in the purchase price leaves the buyer at risk for their realization. The buyer bears the realization risk unless some form of risk-sharing arrangement is negotiated, such as a contingent payment or earn-out (see Section 5.3.4, below).

A classic oversimplification of the modeling of synergies is present when the independent financial advisor makes a conscious decision to model the risk of synergy achievement in the discount rate as opposed to the expected case cash flows. The premise for this oversimplification is that with no explicit cash flow adjustment for the risk that the synergies may not be achieved, projections of the entity are inherently more risky. The discount rate may need to be adjusted upward to reflect the additional risk.

The difficulty lies in determining the amount of the discount rate adjustment and application. In practice, adjusting discount rates to account for such risk is extremely subjective and technically problematic. One major—but most likely unintended—result of this type of adjustment is that *all* forecasted cash flows of the subject business are then assumed to carry this risk, and do so into perpetuity. As a result of the subjective application of such an approach, it is highly recommended that the risk of the projected synergies be dealt with within in the derivation of expected cash flow.

An example of one way the independent financial advisor can summarize the impact of specific modeling changes and adjustments is illustrated in Figure 5–1. In this case, L Co. and V Co. are merging. The value each company is contributing depends on the scenario. The analysis is conducted for the benefit of the board of L Co. The financial projections prepared by the management of L Co. are based upon optimistic assumptions when compared to benchmark data and history, whereas V Co.'s assumptions have been deemed to represent an expected or middle case.

5.3.3 Market/Revenue Synergies

A categorized list of synergies often identified in transactions is presented below. Many of these will sound familiar. What might not sound as familiar are some of the "desynergies" that may be overlooked by management and advisors analyzing the deal. A summary of such "desynergies" is provided directly below each synergy description.

FIGURE 5-1

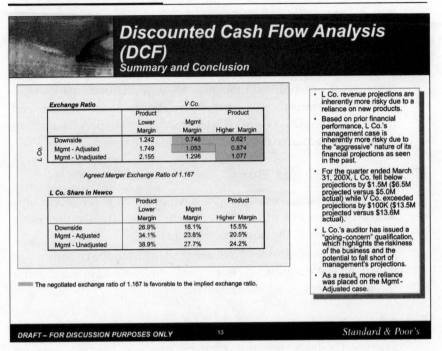

Discounted Cash Flow Analysis (DCF)
Summary and Conclusion

Exchange Ratio — V Co.

L Co.

	Product Lower Margin	Mgmt Margin	Product Higher Margin
Downside	1.242	0.748	0.621
Mgmt - Adjusted	1.749	1.053	0.874
Mgmt - Unadjusted	2.155	1.298	1.077

Agreed Merger Exchange Ratio of 1.167

L Co. Share in Newco

	Product Lower Margin	Mgmt Margin	Product Higher Margin
Downside	26.9%	18.1%	15.5%
Mgmt - Adjusted	34.1%	23.8%	20.5%
Mgmt - Unadjusted	38.9%	27.7%	24.2%

The negotiated exchange ratio of 1.167 is favorable to the implied exchange ratio.

- L Co. revenue projections are inherently more risky due to a reliance on new products.
- Based on prior financial performance, L Co.'s management case is inherently more risky due to the "aggressive" nature of its financial projections as seen in the past.
- For the quarter ended March 31, 200X, L Co. fell below projections by $1.5M ($6.5M projected versus $5.0M actual) while V Co. exceeded projections by $100K ($13.5M projected versus $13.6M actual).
- L Co.'s auditor has issued a "going-concern" qualification, which highlights the riskiness of the business and the potential to fall short of management's projections.
- As a result, more reliance was placed on the Mgmt - Adjusted case.

Broader Product Portfolio

Synergy: An acquirer may be looking to round out the company's product portfolio. There are multiple dimensions to this. An example is a company filling out a product line in a single product category. In the computer industry, a provider of servers geared to small business may add servers geared to large corporations. Another example is providing complementary products. A provider of servers adds storage devices to become more of a "one-stop shop." In the past, the one-stop shop concept was a common and popular synergy. The expected result of this concept is a boost in revenue from an expanded customer base and cross-selling opportunities.

Desynergy: Product lines are not always truly complementary or supplementary. Rationalization of product lines may be required to avoid marketplace confusion and may result in short-term customer dissatisfaction. There may be branding issues. Training sales and service personnel on new products often takes longer than anticipated to accomplish and costs more to implement than projected.

More and/or Broader Distribution Channels

Synergy: The target may provide opportunities to expand traditional distribution channels, such as retail stores. Core distribution may be supplemented through acquisition of a mail order or an Internet-based sales platform.

Desynergy: Certain distributors may have strong relationships with other major competitors. Distributor relationships are valuable and fragile, and the erosion of such relationships may impact the ultimate success of alternative distribution channel expansion.

Broader Customer Base

Synergy: The target company may have contracts and relationships with customers that the acquirer does not have. The acquirer plans to expand sales to the acquired relationships.

Desynergy: Customers may have been buying from the target because they don't like the acquirer. Now that the target is part of the acquirer, those customers may look elsewhere.

Brand Leverage

Synergy: The target may not command premium pricing even with a superior product because of a weak brand. The application of a strong brand to a wider array of products can be a boost to revenue.

Desynergy: There is potential for the buyer to "cheapen" the market's perception of value for the seller's brand by leveraging it too much (e.g., using a luxury brand to market nonluxury goods).

Reduction in Administrative and Other Corporate Overhead Costs

Synergy: This is a classic synergy identified in deals and easy to quantify. The synergy savings is expressed as the opportunity to reduce head count in functions that become redundant in the combined company. For example, companies do not need two CFOs. Executive management, finance, human resources, sales and marketing, legal, and so on, are all areas where head count is typically reduced.

Desynergy: There is always a cost associated with head-count reductions, such as severance and other "soft" costs, that are not always considered part of the "cost of the deal." Merging two distinct corporate cultures may introduce other inefficiencies that are rarely quantified, but can often contribute significantly to poor post-transaction performance.

Manufacturing Efficiency

Synergy: Plant consolidation can yield significant savings through better utilization of assets and plant capacity. Best-in-class processes can be employed in one plant to improve yield, throughput, and, ultimately, the unit cost of production.

Desynergy: Realization of manufacturing cost savings often involve additional investment, whether it be plant closing costs, reconfiguration of production lines, and capital for new equipment or new processes. The transition may introduce short-term reductions in efficiency that managers seldom expect or factor into financial models. Labor costs may actually go up in the short term. For example, the acquirer's plants may utilize a unionized labor force, whereas the target's operation did not.

Purchasing Synergy

Synergy: This is another popular synergy that is relatively straightforward to quantify. The assumption is that with increased size comes increased leverage with suppliers, or, at a minimum, getting the best terms and conditions among similar supply contracts that the acquirer and target have with suppliers.

Desynergy: The combined company may now have volume requirements that cannot be addressed by the existing supplier network, resulting in incremental costs to seek replacement or incremental supply sources.

5.3.4 Earn-Outs

Because synergistic value plays a critical role in many transactions, and because of the incongruity of a "certain" purchase price and "uncertain" synergy value, transactions are often structured with earn-outs (or earn-ins, as the case may be) to better align the interests of both buyer and seller. In a fairness analysis, the independent financial advisor must understand and address the implications of an earn-out. The analysis should include quantification of the value implications both if the earn-out is not achieved and if it is achieved.

In an earn-out, the seller is compensated only when certain financial targets are met. This protects the buyer from paying for value anticipated but yet to be realized. The earn-out has other benefits, including the motivational factors inherent in a contingency-based situation: The selling management is more likely to work hard once the deal has closed. An earn-out spreads the risk inherent in the transaction between the buyer and seller. If expectations are realized, then both sides realize the benefits.

Earn-outs have their downside as well. If the performance measurements are not designed carefully, they may be subject to manipulation or basic measurability problems leading to accounting uncertainty and disputes. There is also the inherent conflict of separating realizable performance expectations from aggressive goals when assessing the buyer's overall financial and operating performance. Earn-outs are typically limited to smaller, nonpublic deals. "Contingency terms are found in 4 percent of all announced U.S. deals—closer to 10 percent of deals valued at or below $250 million. More than 200 acquisitions have contained earn-outs in each of the last five years . . . "[2]

NOTES

1. This is based on the target's closing market price five business days before the initial announcement. These calculations exclude negative premia. Mergerstat Review 2004, FactSet Mergerstat, LLC (2004).

2. "Caution, Earnouts Ahead," Roy Harris, *CFO Magazine*, CFO. com, June 3, 2002.

CHAPTER 6

Valuation Analysis in Special Situations

This chapter provides an overview of some special situations that the independent financial advisor may encounter in a fairness opinion project.

6.1 THIN TRADING EFFECT

In general, transaction prices from active markets are one of the "gold standards" as indicators of market value. When the market is inactive, however, the reliability that can be placed on such prices is limited. This is the "thin trading" problem. Lack of attention to this issue has been the cause of more than one faulty transaction value analysis. Where trading is inadequate, it is not clear whether observed prices are too high, just right, or too low. The independent financial advisor and fiduciary must resist the temptation to take them as either upper or lower bounds. A decision not to rely on market prices due to thin trading problems must be taken carefully and be supportable. Where thin trading is a concern, value indications should be established by other means; for example, through the income approach.

Thin trading occurs if volumes and frequencies are insufficient to respond to market or industry developments on a real-time basis. The only way information can be imputed in prices is via active trading by parties that possess the information. For example, companies subject to lots of news may require more trading for prices to accurately reflect value than companies with little or no news.

Factors to assess and evaluate thin trading include:

- Average daily volume compared to public float of comparable companies (e.g., other companies in the industry).
- Distribution of trading across days (evenly distributed trades versus trades in a couple of spikes).
- Bid-ask spreads: Large spreads call into question the ability of the market to process information about the security.

- Trading fees, taxes, regulations that may inhibit frequent trading.
- Analyst coverage: broad, active, insightful or not.
- Price volatility compared to actively traded comparable companies.
- Identify news events for subject companies and see whether they correlate to spikes in volume and prices.

When circumstances warrant, a detailed review and disclosure of recent changes and trends in a company's share price and trading activity should be incorporated into the analysis. An example of this type of analysis can be seen in Figure 6–1. Each of the notations along the price trend graph is accompanied by a detailed disclosure of relevant information released by the company proximate to the pricing date. This data, along with the related disclosures, allows the analyst to form a qualitative view about how the market is responding to new information about the issuer.

6.2 INTELLECTUAL PROPERTY

Intellectual property (IP) is an increasingly important component of value in transactions. As a result, the independent financial advisor needs to identify, understand, and value IP, either on a stand-alone basis or as part of a going concern.

6.2.1 Definition of Intellectual Property

IP is an asset without tangible form, such as patents or copyrights, as opposed to plant, property, and equipment. Intellectual property may or may not be protected, or be able to be protected, by the legal rights recognized by a governmental entity. From an accounting perspective, to classify an intangible asset as IP, the asset must be identifiable and separable from other assets employed in a business, and possess certain attributes. The asset should:

- Be specifically identifiable and have a recognizable description
- Be subject to the right of private ownership, which must be legally transferable
- Have some tangible evidence of existence
- Have been created or come into existence at an identifiable time or as a result of an identifiable event

FIGURE 6-1

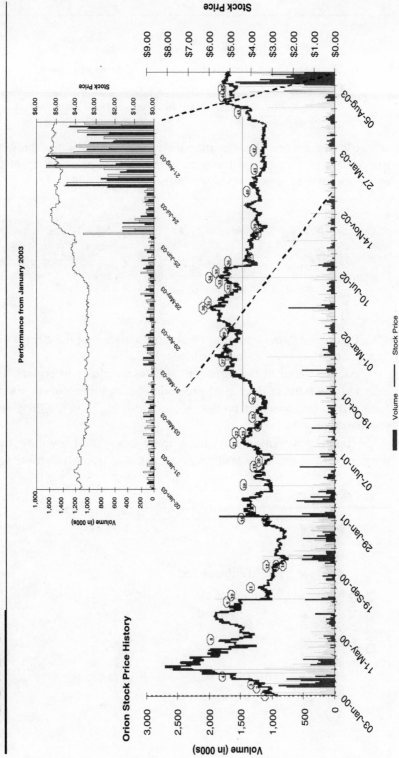

- ♦ Generate some measurable amount of economic benefit to its owner
- ♦ Be able to enhance the value of other assets with which it is associated

Moving beyond the accounting perspective, intellectual property in the context of a proposed transaction can consist of a variety of assets employed by a business, as shown in the following table.

Custom Software	Patents	Trade Names/Trademarks
Customer Lists	Supply Contracts	Assembled Workforce
Formulas	Proprietary Processes/ Trade Secrets	Copyrights

Figure 6–2 provides a graphical representation of the degree of protection afforded to different categories of IP.

As illustrated in the figure, IP such as patents and copyrights are afforded the highest degree of protection as they are documented and filed with governmental bodies, to provide the owner with a legally enforceable right of use.[1]

There are categories of IP, such as trade secrets and know-how, that are not protected in the same fashion. Some valuable IP, such as trade secrets,

FIGURE 6-2

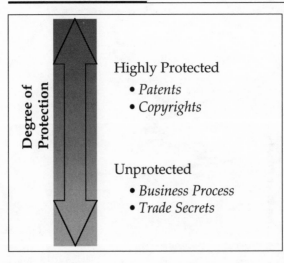

which could be legally registered, commonly remain unregistered to reduce the likelihood of copying. Well-known examples of trade secrets are the Coca-Cola formula and the Mrs. Fields Cookie recipe. Unprotected IP is troublesome in that it is difficult to identify, protect, and value. Although these examples constitute bona fide trade secrets, some sellers may use the guise of "trade secrets" to infer value where it does not exist. The sophisticated buyer is advised to conduct the appropriate due diligence procedures to even the scales a bit in terms of caveat emptor (let the buyer beware).

6.2.2 Due Diligence

Due diligence for IP aims to validate the existence of IP and to identify any risks that may impair its value. The impairment risk should include a determination as to whether (1) there is full ownership of the IP; (2) there are any restrictive provisions surrounding the IP, such as on the scope of use or geographic restrictions; and (3) the transferability of the IP. Because of the legal rights inherent in IP, due diligence may require special legal counsels' assistance.

Ownership

Ownership is illustrated by the patent, which is typically issued to the inventor. Due diligence procedures surrounding patents must be conducted to understand the degree of ownership interest of the seller in the patent. For example, diligence procedures should ensure that proper assignments of the inventor's rights to the patents have been made to the selling organization. Such assignments would be recorded in the U.S. Patent and Trademark Office (USPTO). When multiple inventors share an undivided interest in the patent, all of the inventors have to assign the rights of the patent to the seller. Inventors may leave an organization prior to assigning such rights and may not have an obligation to assign the rights to the selling organization. In such cases, the IP in question would be less valuable than if it were owned in its entirety.

Ownership is further illustrated in situations in which IP is jointly developed by two or more business entities, either in a joint venture or through a cost-sharing arrangement. An example of this occurs in the defense industry. When the U.S. government or a governmental agency funds IP development, the government often grants development rights to several contractors, synthetically creating a competitive environment for its development. In such cases, a company may not have exclusive ownership rights to the IP developed.

Restrictions on Use and Transfer

The value of any asset is enhanced by the owner's ability to use or transfer it without restriction. Due diligence for IP should include understanding any limitations placed on the scope of the IP. For example, a noncompete agreement may limit a patent's application to one commercial area. Any geographic restrictions on the IP, such as a marketing license that may only be used to sell products in the Northeast region of the United States, versus a worldwide license, would impair the license's value. Limitations on the transferability of the IP, including restrictions on the ability to sublicense, affect its value.

Infringement

In addition to the ownership, use, and transferability characteristics of IP, an investigation should also be conducted on IP infringement. In the 1990s, many ownership rights to trademarks were being infringed with the proliferation of the World Wide Web. The Internet became a breeding ground for the opportunistic misappropriation of trademarks using Internet domain names, essentially holding the trademarks hostage. The owners of the infringed trademarks found themselves with the dilemma of diluted brands that could be significantly damaged by their exploitation by others. The traditional rules of IP protection proved insufficient to protect the existing rights in the trademark holders. These rules were recently expanded to restore their validity. Any buyer looking to acquire a company or asset that benefited from exploiting these infringed trademarks should understand the contribution of the exploited IP to the company's business, because that benefit may not exist in the future.

Integration

From a buyer's perspective, due diligence should include an assessment of any potential risks that may arise from integrating the IP into the buyer's business or otherwise exploiting the acquired IP. Although a specific IP asset may seem to be an attractive opportunity, a buyer must gauge how the IP will fit into its platform.

6.2.3 The IP Transaction

Fiduciaries may request a fairness opinion on an IP transaction. In certain industries, such as in the high-tech, biotechnology, or pharmaceutical industries, IP may be the sole asset of high value in a transaction. Certain types of IP transactions are equivalent to a sale because the transaction provides the buying party with all the rights and benefits of ownership. IP transactions include licenses, leasing, royalty agreements, swaps, sharing, and joint development.

Some of the most common objectives underlying an IP transaction include:

- Strengthening an IP portfolio and competitive position
- Improving existing products or services
- Cost reduction; e.g., process improvement, vertical integration of IP that acts as an input into one's products or services
- Increasing revenues through licensing the IP post-transaction
- Broadening corporate "reach" through virtualization

The review process around a transaction that involves IP is often different from the process used for tangible assets. The independent financial advisor will most likely require a higher degree of confidence before rendering an opinion of fairness on an IP transaction. In the case of a transaction involving IP, confidence can depend on the degree of protection afforded to the IP. As discussed in earlier chapters, confidence can be obtained through more detailed due diligence and by relying on more valuation reference points. Stand-alone IP deals may be fair; however, there may be instances where the independent financial advisor cannot get a satisfactory level of confidence to render a fairness opinion.

6.2.4 IP as Part of an Ongoing Business

The independent financial advisor will have more confidence in valuing IP as part of a going concern that has a proven track record, as compared to valuing IP in isolation.

The value of IP plays an increasingly important role in justifying the purchase price paid for an ongoing business. This is especially true in cases in which the value of the business significantly exceeds its book value. Balance sheets do not reflect the value of organically developed IP. A separate analysis should be conducted to reconcile the estimated purchase price to the underlying tangible and intangible assets of the business. This analysis is often combined with a buyer's preliminary assessment of the dilutive impact of the amortization of intangible assets under SFAS No. 141. To reconcile a purchase price, the advisor may extend the analysis beyond those assets that are recognizable under SFAS No. 141 accounting rules.

6.2.5 IP Valuation

In a transaction whose primary value driver resides in the IP that is being exchanged, fiduciaries should be aware of the issues surrounding the value ascribed to the IP. When determining whether the transaction is fair, the fiduciary should ensure that these issues are properly addressed and incorporated in the value assessment.

Valuation Approaches

As discussed in Chapter 4, there are several approaches to valuing an asset: the income approach, the market approach, and the cost approach. A most common approach employed in valuing IP is the relief-from-royalty method, a hybrid between the income and market approaches. Other approaches to value IP may include:

- ◆ A relative valuation, based on comparable IP transactions (market approach)
- ◆ An analysis of the premium profits associated with the IP (income approach)
- ◆ Analysis of the cost to develop the IP (cost approach)

Applying a market approach to value IP is often difficult, since the terms of IP transactions are not typically disclosed to the open market-place. However, certain research firms track data relating to IP transactions in their industry. This data may provide a reasonable benchmark to use in a valuation of some forms of IP.

Other factors taken into account in estimating the value of the IP may be:

- ◆ Relative strength of the IP
- ◆ Protection afforded to the IP
- ◆ Implications of the IP on profitability
- ◆ Market share resulting from owning or using the IP
- ◆ Nature of the market (industrial, manufacturing, retail, etc.)

6.2.6 Relief-from-Royalty Valuation Method

The underlying premise of the relief-from-royalty method is that the value of the IP is equal to the cost savings or royalty avoided resulting from ownership of the IP. In other words, the owner of the IP will realize a benefit from owning the IP by not paying a rent or royalty charge for its use to third parties.

The relief-from-royalty method requires the projection of the expected revenues attributable to the IP for the duration that the IP is expected to remain commercially viable. A benchmarked royalty rate that a third party would pay to license the IP is estimated based on observed arm's length royalties for comparable licensed IP. This royalty rate is estimated to be the amount that a licensor and licensee would negotiate if both had reasonably and voluntarily attempted to reach agreement. The royalty rate is then applied to the projected revenue stream for the IP to determine the projected royalty expense that the owner of the IP avoids. The projected royalty expense avoided is discounted to estimate the present value of the IP. Further adjustments may be warranted for restrictions, infringement, or partial interests.

Sources to be used in determining an appropriate royalty rate are:

+ Third-party royalty rates for comparable licensed IP. This information may be obtained from searching the databases developed from public information on royalty agreements.

+ Royalty rates for comparable IP already licensed. The company may already have licensing agreements with third parties for the subject IP or IP that is reasonably comparable. These agreements may be used as a benchmark to estimate a hypothetical royalty rate for the subject IP. However, an advisor should be aware that licensing agreements often have restrictive provisions with regard to the industry sectors and/or regions in which they may be used, and should adjust these rates to reflect a rate that would be commensurate with all the rights and benefits of ownership.

+ Rules of thumb, which typically involve the assumption of "what the market will bear." A benchmark based on the operating margin of a typical licensee can be used to estimate the maximum rate the licensee would bear to pay for the IP. Some benchmarks assume that a licensee would normally bear anywhere between 25 and 33 percent of their operating margin. These benchmarks are very general. In some industries, royalty rates may be much higher or lower than this benchmark.

+ Primary market research, which is often deemed cost-prohibitive and/or too time consuming for fairness opinions.

While the relief-from-royalty method is widely used, it is fraught with potential error and potentially understates the value of owned IP.

For example, valuing a trademark using the royalty savings method may undervalue the trademark because a licensee has less control over the use of a trademark than a trademark owner has; an analysis based exclusively on licensing royalty rates necessarily understates the fair market value of trademarks.

The fair market value of a trademark is the price a willing purchaser would have paid in an arm's length transaction. The relief-from-royalty method may not accurately estimate the value to the purchaser of a trademark.

> A relief-from-royalty model fails to capture the value of all of the rights of ownership, such as the power to determine when and where a mark may be used, or moving a mark into or out of product lines . . . Ownership of a mark is more valuable than a license because ownership carries with it the power and incentive both to put the mark to its most valued use and increase its value. A licensee cannot put the mark to use beyond the temporal or other limitations of a license and has no reason to take steps to increase the value of a mark where the increased value will be realized by the owner. [2]

A trademark license is not as valuable as ownership because it may include provisions restricting the use of the trademark (e.g., to only certain products or markets) and may be limited in time.

In the case of trademarks, a firm may be able to make additional sales or charge a premium price without a commensurate increase in costs. The typical application of the relief-from-royalty method begins with a search for arm's length license agreements for use of "comparable" trademarks. These "comparables" often reflect start-up products or market extensions where royalty rates would tend to be lower.

Seasoned (well-established) trademarks have developed a "goodwill" value of their own. Under trademark law, a trademark may be sold or assigned only with the goodwill of the business in which the trademark is used. Trademark value should include associated goodwill value. Even though under a license agreement a licensee is paying a licensor for use of the goodwill, the agreements used are often entered into before the goodwill of the trademark has been established (or established for a specific product or in a specific geographic area), and, therefore, understates the royalty that a licensee of the trademark would be willing to pay (or a licensor would charge) for a license of a seasoned trademark.

Even then, valuing trademarks only by reference to license royalties necessarily undervalues the trademarks because the licensor retains legal ownership of the goodwill associated with the trademarks.

With regard to technology assets (whether patented or not patented), we often have much the same problem. Arm's length license agreements often are entered into prior to (or do not include) the full development of the application of the technology. The licensee often must invest considerable monies taking the kernel of the technology received in a typical patent license and building his or her own tested and proven application of the kernel to the product or process. A purchaser of the technology gets the equivalent benefit of both the license use of the basic technology and the application. A purchaser of a fully developed technology gets more value than represented by the typical license.

6.3 THE ROLL-UP STRATEGY

This section addresses the valuation issues arising from a roll-up or market consolidation strategy transaction. The capital markets credit the consolidator with a strategy of deriving higher value from amalgamating a number of players in a fragmented market. The consolidator creates value by acquiring companies at lower valuation multiples than the multiple at which the consolidator will trade. The difference in pricing can be attributable, in part, to the premium awarded to the consolidator for anticipated synergies.

6.3.1 Arbitrage

Roll-up transactions often involve an arbitrage in value. When an asset trades at different prices in different markets and the spread is greater than the transaction costs, a pure arbitrage exists. A simultaneous trade in the two markets will produce a certain profit. Roll-up transactions appear to have some elements of arbitrage since the increase in value of the buyer/consolidator will exceed the price of the target entity. The market rewards the consolidator by valuing it at a higher multiple than the independent enterprise. The resulting value can allow the consolidator to generate returns that are comparable to those seen in pure arbitrage.

Roll-ups, however, are not pure arbitrage because the consolidated entity must deliver the economic results to sustain the market values. When a consolidator consolidates then sells out prior to achieving the anticipated operating results, arbitrage occurs.

For the fiduciary of either the buyer or seller in a roll-up transaction, an understanding of the values and options of all parties is helpful in determining whether their interests are being treated fairly.

6.3.2 Consolidator/Buyer

The market looks to see that the consolidator (1) has a strategy to build critical mass through acquisition and integration, (2) can unlock value through operating efficiency and economics of scale, and (3) can effectively execute the strategy. An example of improved economics is the ability to service larger customers, resulting in increased revenues and lower unit costs per dollar of revenue generated. See Section 5.3 for a discussion on synergies.

The challenge in the fairness opinion analysis for the consolidator is to balance the price and value of the target with the value implications to the consolidator. The price and value of the target is quantified in standard fashion. The consolidator's valuation in a consolidation strategy may be driven by factors other than cash flow or net income growth. Often the market value anticipates the consolidator's achievement of synergies in the roll-up. The market uses matrices reflecting this anticipation in its consolidated pricing multiples. These higher multiples need to be reflected in the market value analysis of the consolidator. At some point the market will expect the consolidator's operating results to support the market value.

The projected operating results and DCF models will include the anticipated synergies resulting from consolidation of the proposed target and the risk of achieving those synergies. Discount rates may need to be adjusted to reflect any change in the level of market risk due to the consolidation. The resulting change in value of the consolidator can then be compared to the price/value of the target entity. For the roll-up strategy to work, the consolidator's change in value should be higher than the price of the target.

For example, assume the consolidator's market valuation is three times its current revenue. It acquires a company at a value of one times revenue. For every dollar paid for a dollar of revenue, three dollars of market capitalization is potentially created in the perceived value of the consolidator.

Case Study: Eagle Acquisition by Cardinal

Eagle operated in two distinct segments of the pharmacy business: the retail segment and the institutional segment. Prior to its sale to Cardinal, Eagle operated nine retail stores and provided pharmacy products and services to approximately 15 long-term care facilities in South Central Pennsylvania, servicing approximately 2,800 long-term care beds at a run rate of approximately $2,300 of revenue per bed serviced.

At the time Cardinal was negotiating with Eagle, the pharmacy services sector was in the midst of major consolidation. In the case of Cardinal and other publicly traded industry consolidators, the open market valuations averaged 2.7 times total revenue, or $4,900 times the number of long-term care beds serviced. The consolidator was acquiring the small target companies for an average of 1.0 times total institutional revenue, or $2,400 times long-term care beds serviced.

Under the original $10.3 million purchase price, Cardinal's market value was enhanced by approximately $27.0 million. This value increase, if fully ascribed to the Eagle acquisition, yielded a return of roughly 130 percent based upon the spread between Cardinal's trading revenue multiple and the implied revenue multiple to be paid for Eagle.

The concept of sharing potential market capitalization is another issue for the independent financial advisor to investigate and communicate to the fiduciary in roll-up transactions. The value of the stand-alone target is usually less than the potential value to the consolidator. Many targets will have little pricing leverage. In these cases, the consolidator makes a "take it or leave it" type offer. At different stages of a consolidation, a target may have pricing leverage and may demand to share in the increase in value the consolidator will enjoy. In effect, the price of the target may show a premium to the target's stand-alone value. This is an analogous situation to synergy sharing discussed in Chapter 5. The independent financial advisor should consider this dynamic and share his or her views with the fiduciary body.

The fiduciary should understand the consolidation rationale and how the proposed transaction aids in achieving the rationale. Failure to achieve the consolidation rationale risks a reversal of value that is often disproportionate to the value of the proposed transaction. The pricing of the proposed transaction may be fair, but the incremental risk of failure to achieve the consolidation strategy—and the resulting market value reduction—may make the transaction questionable. In most fairness opinions, the balance of value used in the analysis will not address the risk of strategy failure. Yet the fiduciary must consider this possibility during deliberations on whether to approve the transaction.

6.3.3 The Seller in a Roll-Up Scenario

The independent financial advisor for the seller in a roll-up transaction approaches the fairness question as he or she would any other transaction opportunity. The proposed terms will be weighed against the values of the interests to be surrendered in the sale.

Liquidity opportunities play a role in the independent financial advisor's analysis of fairness. Another value to the seller is the ability to convert an illiquid interest into a liquid interest. While liquidity is a factor in the basic valuation used for a fairness analysis, the creation of liquidity adds a value to the seller that the independent financial advisor should fully explore.

Other factors may affect the independent financial advisor's analysis from the seller's perspective. The sum of the values allocated to partial ownership interests does not always equal the value of the whole enterprise. At the same time, liquidity events where the value of the whole enterprise can be realized are not always available. Roll-up transactions often provide superior returns to the consolidator for the elimination of dysfunctional structures. The minority interests may not have value realization options beyond the roll-up offer. The Company B case illustrates the complexity of evaluating illiquid minority interests.

Case Study: Company B

Company B, a private equity firm, pursued a strategy of aggregating real estate limited partnerships and converting the consolidated group into a publicly traded REIT. Each partnership was comprised of a general partner that effectively had control and several limited partners, similar in this case to minority shareholders. The private equity sponsor was concerned about fair treatment of all tendering LP unit holders notionally the sellers in the transaction.

In the process of combining these entities under one umbrella, the private equity firm encountered several issues. One issue pertained to the relative valuation of each partnership and LP interest considering the location of properties in the portfolio, their income-generating potential, and other characteristics.

The second issue encountered by the private equity firm was the relative distribution of REIT shares between general and limited partners (LP), considering control and minority issues. The pre-roll-up structure had one general partner and nine LPs with equal stakes. The partnership structure created an impact on value from the LPs' perspective. The value of the interests of the LPs was worth less than their proportional share of the total. The interest of the general partner was worth at least its proportional share of the partnership's net assets. In the roll-up transaction, LPs were diluted in a larger structure. However, since the combined vehicle was taken public, the value of their interests in the larger structure were greater than the LP interest due to increased marketability. A central question for the independent financial advisor was: "Is this trade-off fair to the LP?"

Based upon its analysis, the trade-off was demonstrated to be fair. The transaction was ultimately perceived to be fair by the LPs, and the transaction closed under the terms offered by the private equity firm. In evaluating the reasonableness of this transaction, the LPs considered not only the underlying value of the real estate, but also the relevant marketability considerations and an assessment of the probability or likelihood of another liquidity event occurring. See Section 7.2.4 for a discussion on marketability discounts.

Beyond the role of the fairness opinion, the fiduciary for the seller in a roll-up proposal will wrestle with other issues. Two issues are covered here because they tend to be interwoven in the financial analysis. The fiduciary should be aware of any arbitrage potential to the consolidator. The fact that an arbitration opportunity exists for the consolidator is probably not a factor in the seller's ultimate decision. That the consolidator can create more value than the price after the transaction is to be expected. The fiduciary for the seller must also consider the integration risk, if part of the consideration received is a continued interest in the consolidator. The values ascribed to the entity post-transaction may not be realized, even if the entity achieves the forecasted results used to determine value. The market may change its value perceptions. These risks associated with the sustainability of the value should be weighed by the fiduciary.

6.4 EARLY STAGE COMPANIES

Transactions involving early stage companies pose unique issues for the independent financial advisor. Early stage companies are those entities whose businesses have yet to achieve the operating characteristics typically associated with a sustainable going concern. In most cases the business plan or premise is unproven. Often these companies are exploring potentially attractive new opportunities in the market through joint ventures or other alliances that have been newly formed and lack a proven track record. There are few comparable transactions to use as a basis for analyzing investments in such companies. Where the business concept is new, there may be little established public data or market pricing for the relevant technology or operating model.

Early stage company transactions fall into several categories including:

- Cash-constrained, poorly performing companies seeking critical additional funding
- Cash-constrained companies that are on plan seeking critical additional funding
- Well-funded start-ups seeking to acquire critical elements or building blocks for their business model
- Sales of noncore proprietary technology to fund core activities
- Ownership sharing to establish essential technology or business relationships
- Other business relationships typically designed to preserve cash, execute the business model, and improve the probability of achieving going concern status

Transactions involving cash-constrained, poorly performing companies seeking to obtain additional financing pose their own special valuation and fairness issues. The risk is high that the additional funds may not allow the business model to achieve going concern status. Without additional funds, the entity will most likely cease to exist. Comparing the value of the consideration received to the interest given up involves speculative elements. The methodologies employed by the independent financial advisor to address such uncertainty are critical to the fairness analysis.

Transactions involving companies obtaining additional financing to further the development of a business plan that is on track pose a different series of issues for the independent financial advisor. These companies need additional funds but are on or close to plan. Potential new money is still required and creates dilution of existing interests. Existing investors may not have equivalent interest in the entity and thus would not be equally affected by the dilution. In the fairness analysis, the independent financial advisor should understand any shifts in interests and the related value implications.

Investors in early stage companies may require more than just a financial interest in the capital structure of the business. Specifically, new investors may require preferential financial treatment, conversion rights, public registration and listing rights, board seats and voting preferences. These preferences and rights have value that must be considered by the independent financial advisor. The independent financial advisor analyzing the transaction should provide a full briefing of the financial ramifications of investor preferences and rights and the way in which they were modeled.

In most instances, multiple rounds of financing for early stage companies result in increasingly complex capital structures. Past valuations cannot be the sole basis for deciding whether a proposed transaction is fair. Early stage companies' values change very rapidly. The value in the most recent round of financing is not a sufficient basis for the value in the proposed round of financing. A fresh analysis needs to be undertaken for each new transaction.

An early stage company in its growth cycle poses other valuation challenges. These include consideration of alternatives to the proposed transaction, the weaknesses of comparable companies and market/technology/industry data, and the risk inherent in the business plan given its stage of development. In today's world, the early stage company analysis may be closer to the type of analysis employed when valuing pure intellectual property assets, rather than valuing a business that employs such assets. Intellectual property transactions are covered in Section 6.2.

6.5 CO-OPS AND NOT-FOR-PROFITS

Co-ops and not-for-profits pose unique valuation challenges to the independent financial advisor in conducting a fairness analysis. Within the past 10 years the pace at which businesses that are notionally owned by suppliers, customers, and not-for-profit organizations have been sold or converted to stock form of ownership has increased. The rationale often cited for transactions is access to capital to better facilitate competitiveness, growth, or mission achievement. A number of states have initiated legislative oversight measures in connection with corporate conversions, sales, and going public transactions involving not-for-profit businesses.

Recent events have demonstrated that co-ops and not-for-profits can create shareholder value. [3] In some cases capital has been retained and employed in the activity, creating value. Other values arise from the going concern nature of their activities on behalf of their constituency, including realization of brand value, market power, and scale of activities.

Not-for-profit businesses create fundamental challenges to traditional valuation tools. The implicit assumption is cash flow modeling and market-based valuation approaches. This may not be valid. The not-for-profit may be using some measure other than profitability to keep score. Instead of profitability, the entity may measure being "on mission" achieving the objectives of its mission statement or charter.

Activist groups argue in transactions involving tax-exempt entities that the not-for-profit has benefited from a capital investment in the form of foregone taxes. Where there has been volunteer support, activists would argue that the volunteers' foregone income is another form of capital support. Therefore, activists argue society or the taxpayer should share in any benefits arising from a proposed transaction.

Beyond the taxpayer is the interest of the co-op member or mutual association member. This member has utilized the not-for-profit to supply a need. At the same time, the pricing inherent in supplying the services to the members has allowed the organization to develop. In theory, the member is the basis for the organization, and so any enterprise value should flow to the members. Changing members further complicates this consideration.

Legislative initiatives and state oversight departments have tried to address these kinds of issues. For example, states have charged insurance commissioners with the oversight and approval of transactions involving insurance companies registered in their states. Many states have specific regulations for the conversion of policyholder-owned insurance companies to stockholder-owned corporations. The commission will consider whether the proposed transaction complies with insurance regulations designed to protect policyholders and insurance activity in the state. The value of the entity and its allocation among the parties may or may not be defined in these regulations. In some states the regulator or state attorneys general will function in the role of fiduciary for the public and mutual holders. These regulators may request their own fairness opinion.

NOTES

1. An exception to this rule occurs when a patent can be invalidated, if a challenger can prove that the patent has critical defects. Therefore, due diligence should also include an examination of whether a patent meets the subject matter, novelty, utility, and nonobviousness requirements of patent law.

2. *Nestle Holdings, Inc. v. Comm.*, 152 F. 3d 83 (1998).

3. Fonterra Co-operative Group Limited was formed by the merger of three legacy co-operative companies. The new economics that accompanied this merger provided a new capital instrument for the co-operative's suppliers/shareholders that is valued regularly, provides liquidity, and forms a significant part of the suppliers'/shareholders' investment/net worth.

CHAPTER 7

Technical Issues

In this section we briefly introduce a number of technical issues that often arise during the fairness opinion value analysis. These include capital structure issues, discounts and premia, tax considerations, and international risk factors.

7.1 CAPITAL STRUCTURE

Values need to reflect considerations of off-balance-sheet financing, market value of debt, guarantees, operating leases, preferred securities, and stock options.

7.1.1 Off-Balance-Sheet Financing

The last 20 years have seen the introduction of an abundance of new financing vehicles available to companies, many of which may not appear on a company's balance sheet. One response to this trend has been the body of accounting guidance that has emerged to make the impact of such arrangements more transparent in the financial statements. FASB Interpretation No. 46, *Consolidation of Variable Interest Entities* (FIN 46), is one such pronouncement. Although off-balance-sheet financing structures have been used for quite some time, some structures are fairly new and more difficult to analyze. Examples of off-balance-sheet financing arrangements that companies may enter into include:

- *Secured or factored receivables.* Receivables that are sold to third parties for which the company may retain certain liabilities, typically provided for in a recourse provision
- *Certain financial instruments.* Include interest rate swaps, forward contracts, guarantees and commitments, which may not be accounted for, or only partially accounted for, on a company's balance sheet

♦ *Insubstance defeasance of debt.* Securities that are purchased and placed in a trust for the sole purpose of providing timely payments of debt

7.1.2 Market Value of Debt

Elements of a company's capital structure, including debt, impact various aspects of the valuation analysis. Areas where the market value of debt impact the valuation analysis include:

♦ *WACC.* Market values rather than book values should be used to assign weights to the debt, common equity, and preferred equity of a company.

♦ *Allocating BEV to the common equity interests.* Market value of debt and preferred equity should be deducted.

♦ *Guideline company analysis.* In computing normalized valuation multiples and operating parameters, market value of debt should be considered.

♦ *Equity cash flows.* Pro forma interest expense should be calculated using market rates.

Pursuant to SFAS 107 (*Disclosures about Fair Value of Financial Instruments,* December 1991), public companies are required to disclose the fair value of their debt instruments in the footnotes to their financial statements. This analysis becomes more complex for nonpublic entities, which do not have to disclose this information. However, this analysis may still be performed using the company's incremental or marginal borrowing rate to discount their future debt payments.

The independent financial advisor will determine the market value of debt. The steps include:

♦ Determination of timing and magnitude of contractual payments.

♦ Determination of the applicable borrowing rate for an investment with comparable risk characteristics based on market data. Notes to financial statements are instrumental to learn more about company's interest-bearing debt.

♦ Discount future obligations to present value equivalent at the applicable borrowing rate.

7.1.3 Guarantees

The existence and substance of guarantees are something that the independent financial advisor should be prepared to investigate and analyze. The FASB has issued FASB Interpretation No. 45, *Guarantor's Accounting and Disclosure Requirements for Guarantees, Including Indirect Guarantees of Indebtedness of Others* (FIN 45), which requires a company to measure the value of a guarantee made at its inception, and to recognize the value of the guarantee as a liability on its balance sheet. A fiduciary should be sure the independent financial advisor rendering the fairness opinion fully assesses the implications of such guarantees. The recognition of guarantees on a company's balance sheet will impact its capital structure. Such recognition may impair its debt rating and violate certain bond covenants, effectively increasing its cost of debt.

7.1.4 Operating Leases

Some companies capitalize their leases and are required to disclose such information on their balance sheets. In contrast, companies may also have fixed obligations that do not appear on their balance sheets. A common example of this is an operating lease, which is a lease that does not meet the criteria for capitalization for financial reporting purposes under SFAS No. 13, *Accounting for Leases.* Although operating leases are not recognized as liabilities on a company's balance sheet, they nonetheless represent fixed obligations on behalf of the company, and should be regarded as debt when estimating the company's capital structure. Rating agencies consider operating leases as debt in evaluating the creditworthiness of a company. The market is not fooled by the artificial rules accountants use to classify debt.

7.1.5 Preferred Securities

Preferred securities often have liquidation preference. The value impact of features like liquidation preference will depend on prospects for liquidation. The higher this likelihood, the higher the value of preferred in relation to common stock. Option pricing methodologies can be applied in valuing these dynamics.

The recent case of First Union Real Estate Equity and Mortgage Investments, described below, illustrates what can occur if boards do not consider the interests of other investor groups such as the preferred shareholders.

Case Study: First Union Real Estate Equity and Mortgage Investments

First Union Real Estate Equity and Mortgage Investments (FUR), a real estate investment trust, was acquired in a hostile takeover by Gotham Partners, L.P. (Gotham). As a result of the transaction, the preferred shareholders of FUR were converted to notionally equivalent preferred shareholders of Newco, a business with significantly fewer financial resources to provide for the preferred returns or liquidation preference associated with the preferred securities.

The preferred shareholders sued in the Supreme Court of the State of New York and a preliminary injunction was granted. The preferred shareholders alleged that the transaction would essentially force them to "remain shareholders in the newly formed corporation in a greatly disadvantaged position . . . [and] their interest[s] are being sacrificed to the interests of Ackman and/or Gotham because they would be compelled against their will to invest in his failing business."

The Honorable Charles Edward Ramos, J.S.C., presiding over the hearing, indicated that the fairness opinion submitted by FUR's board of trustees to its shareholders "neglect[ed] to opine on the fairness of this transaction to the preferred shareholders." The court considered the failure to be a "significant omission in its evaluation of the entire transaction" and reiterated the duties owed by trustees to *all* the equity holders of FUR to include:

> The obligation to present accurate and candid presentation of the proposed transaction;[1] to safeguard the equity of the preferred;[2] to a fair appointment of merger proceeds;[3] and to advise truthfully the directors' interest and possible conflicts.[4]

7.1.6 Stock Options

Many companies issue stock options to their employees in lieu of or in addition to their cash salaries. In such cases, it may be appropriate to adjust a company's market value of common equity to include the value of its stock options. Such an adjustment may be made using the data outlined in SFAS No. 123, *Accounting for Stock-Based Compensation,* using the value method prescribed. This adjustment would result in a higher proportion of equity in a company's capital structure and would potentially result in a modest impact on the cost of capital. However, the guidance provided by SFAS No. 123 may become obsolete, as a new exposure draft circulating on this issue will likely replace SFAS No. 123 and call for fair value accounting with respect to options.

It should be noted that while such guidance is important to the independent financial advisor, a fair value determination depends on the financial advisor's interpretation of the facts and circumstances, judgment, and technical assessment.

7.1.7 Bondholder Considerations

Directors of a company are generally regarded as having a fiduciary duty to the equity holders. However, they may also have a fiduciary duty to disclose the impact of a potential transaction on bondholders. Bondholders of a company do not have control in the day-to-day operations of the company. The bondholders look to the bond indenture provisions to protect their investments. The bond indenture may require a company to obtain a fairness opinion to the trustee for the bondholders. A key issue for a bondholder fairness opinion is to protect the bondholder from any fraudulent conveyance.

The independent financial advisor may need to consider the fairness of the transaction to all *classes* of investors, including its secured and unsecured debt holders, as well as its preferred shareholders. [5]

7.2 PREMIA AND DISCOUNTS

Once the value of the business has been determined, the focus of the analysis shifts to the specific nature and characteristics of the subject interest. This section discusses the appropriate discounts and/or premia applicable in the valuation analysis.

There are theoretical and economic justifications for the application of various premia and discounts. The laws and customs of some jurisdictions may restrict the level of discounts allowed for certain value analysis. Certain jurisdictions allow both a minority and marketability discount to be applied in a valuation, while other jurisdictions do not. States permitting discounts or other adjustments to be applied in a valuation include New York, Kentucky, Oregon, Colorado, and Georgia.

7.2.1 Control Premium

The level of control inherent in the ownership interest in a private business remains an important consideration in determining value. A company that can be more efficiently managed to achieve synergies in a transaction can command a price above and beyond the investment value under current ownership supporting a controlling interest premium. Some factors to consider in evaluating the level of majority shareholders' control are their ability to:

+ Elect directors
+ Select management
+ Direct dividend policy
+ Establish compensation and benefits
+ Acquire or liquidate assets
+ Compel the sale of a company
+ Liquidate, dissolve, or recapitalize the company
+ Revise the articles and bylaws
+ Place restrictions on an initial public offering (IPO)
+ Affect future earnings
+ Control efforts for growth potential

The control value of a company may not differ greatly and may even be below its publicly traded minority share value. Thus, the facts and circumstances surrounding each proposed transaction should be evaluated in arriving at an appropriate control premium or discount.

The independent financial advisor must consider if a control premium may already be partially in the public stock price if the target was "in play." If so, it is more difficult for the independent financial advisor to isolate the control premium because some effect is already present.

If an independent financial advisor determines the control premium for a particular investment to be 20 percent, this does not translate into a minority discount of 20 percent. This is illustrated by the following example.

Control Premium vs. Minority Discount

A private company's equity value is determined to be $200. The company's shareholders are comprised of one shareholder owning 60 percent of its outstanding shares, while many individual investors own the remaining 40 percent of shares. Apportioning the value based on relative ownership percentages results in $120 of value attributed to the majority shareholder, while $80 is attributed to the minority shareholders. Upon analyzing the control characteristics of the majority shareholder's stake, an independent financial advisor attributes a 20 percent control premium to the controlling share. As a result, the majority stake is valued at $144, and the remaining minority value is valued at $56, implying a 30 percent discount from the minority's original pro rata value of $80.

7.2.2 Super-Voting Rights

In transactions involving companies with multiple classes of stock with different voting rights, consideration should be given to whether a premium is warranted for the superior voting rights of one class of stock over another. This is a separate issue from that of the control exercisable over a business by its majority shareholders.

Companies employing a dual-class ownership structure usually have one class of stock with superior voting power over another. Examples of companies with dual-class stock with differential voting rights are Ford Motor Company, Comcast, Cox Communications, The New York Times Co., Dow Jones & Co., and Viacom. The Ford family controls 40 percent of shareholder voting power with only about 5.5 percent of the total equity in the company through its ownership of Class B shares.

Most empirical evidence regarding the value of a voting premium is not clear due to the other circumstances relating to specific companies that may influence their values. It is widely suggested that the premium given to additional voting rights of stock is more a product of the controlling influence of the shares rather than the sole privilege for voting; that is, if the vote has little influence over the operations or control of a company, then little premium is warranted.

A tax court case provides some evidence of the difficulty in assessing a premium for superior voting rights. In the case of *The Estate of Simplot v. Commissioner of Internal Revenue,* the tax court held that "the class A shares (voting), on a per-share basis, are far more valuable than the class B (non-voting) shares because of the former's inherent potential for influence and control of the Company." The court adopted a 3 percent premium to the price of the class A shares over the class B shares. However, the Ninth Circuit Court overturned this decision on May 14, 2001, concluding that there should be no voting premium in this particular case for the subject minority ownership position of the class A shares, despite the unequal voting rights.

Several studies looked at the premium for superior voting rights as the shares traded in the ordinary course in the public market.[6] Purchases and sales of shares in a public market represent minority interests, thus a superior voting right of one stock class over another has little value unless enough shares are owned to give voting control. In a transaction, the delivery of voting control and/or transaction effectiveness may create a basis for some superior voting right premium. A variety of studies on this topic affirm the factual nature and rationale for this premium. Therefore, the independent financial advisor will want to qualitatively and quantitatively address this factor, when it is present, and communicate its approach and findings to the fiduciary body as part of the fairness analysis.

7.2.3 Minority Discount

In valuing minority interests, a minority interest discount may be applied to account for the fact that a minority shareholder lacks certain rights and is unable to control the operations of the business or influence management's decision.

The economic considerations that should be applied in determining the appropriate level of minority discount are those that impact the minority shareholders' rights relative to majority shareholders. The level of a minority discount is directly related to the rights afforded to majority shareholders. The greater the control premium attributable to the majority, the greater the discount that should be applied to the remaining interests.

One source of data used to quantify minority interest discounts is on publicly traded companies. The independent financial advisor can derive minority interest discounts using the inverse of data provided in control premium studies as follows:

$$\text{Minority Interest Discount} = 1 - [1/(1 - \text{Control Premium})]$$

Where Control Premium relates to the appropriate control prices in the industry sector.

When using this data, the conversion from controlling interest to minority interest or vice versa is considered before the application of the discount for lack of marketability. In assessing the control premium data, the independent financial advisor must remove the transactions that represent premiums for unique buyer-specific synergies that influenced the price offered and that general market participants would not be able to duplicate. Further, published average control premiums typically omit transaction prices that were less than the speculative market trading prices that may have preceded the transaction announcement. Omitting transactions simply because the convention used by the data service in measuring the premium results in a "negative premiums" may distort the true market pricing.

7.2.4 Marketability Discount

The American Society of Appraisers defines a marketability discount as "an amount or percentage deducted from the value of an ownership interest to reflect the relative inability to quickly convert property to cash."

In addition to a minority discount, a marketability discount may also be appropriate in the valuation of a minority interest. Investors prefer investments that have access to a liquid secondary market and may be readily converted into cash. Equity interests without such marketability and liquidity characteristics normally sell at a discount in order to provide the investor with compensation for this lack of liquidity.

The discount for lack of marketability considers the absence of a readily available market for the subject interest relative to the markets for the securities to which the subject interest is being compared. This discount is a function of the costs that would be incurred to improve liquidity, including the uncertain time horizon to complete a sale and the cost of a sale or liquidation (i.e., auditing/accounting fees, legal fees, administrative costs, transaction and brokerage fees) and the time it takes to sell such an interest.

The jurisdiction of the company is a primary consideration in determining whether such a discount is appropriate. Factors to consider in establishing a discount for lack of marketability: [7]

1. Financial condition of the company
2. Company's dividend policy
3. History and nature of the company, the industry, and overall economy
4. Company's management
5. Amount of control in the transferred shares
6. Any restrictions on transferability
7. The holding period
8. Company's redemption policy
9. Costs associated with a public offering

Various databases with historical data of actual prices paid for nonliquid shares are available. The independent financial advisor needs to assess the appropriateness of that data in drawing conclusions as to a marketability discount appropriate for the subject interest.

7.3 TAX ISSUES

7.3.1 Pass-Through Entities

One of the most contentious valuation issues is that of determining the value of interests in pass-through entities. Pass-through entities do not pay entity level taxes, relieving them from the double taxation to which C Corporations are subject. Pass-through entities may take a variety of forms, including:

♦ S Corporations

+ Limited liability companies (LLCs)
+ Limited liability partnerships (LLPs)
+ Limited partnerships (LPs)
+ General partnerships (GPs)
+ Real estate investment trusts (REITs)

Although most valuation cases involving pass-through entities have arisen in the tax courts, these cases are instructive. In *Gross v. Commissioner,* the tax court held that small minority interests in G&J Bottling, a large independent Pepsi bottler organized as an S Corporation, should be valued reflecting the tax benefits of an S Corporation rather than those of a C Corporation. The court used the cash flows without subtracting any hypothetical entity level income taxes for the S Corporation as the basis for valuation of the subject's interests. [8] In Delaware Chancery Court the fair value of an interest in a pass-through entity was similarly valued. [9]

The "pool of likely buyers" often held as a key assumption in determining how to value a pass-through entity. Many financial advisors believe that if the entity is being sold in its entirety—i.e., a 100 percent interest—then the likely buyer often is a C Corporation. When applying an income approach to the valuation, the pass-through entity's earnings would be tax-affected at a likely buyer's corporate tax rate. To discount the tax-affected cash flows to the present, a tax-affected weighted average cost of capital would then be applied.

For cases in which a minority interest in a pass-through entity is being valued, the most likely buyer may be a pass-through qualified buyer. This buyer would likely benefit from pass-through tax status. Therefore the income approach valuation of such a minority interest is based on the cash flows without subtracting hypothetical entity level taxes. In these cases, a premium over the value of an interest in an otherwise identical C Corporation may be justified.

The independent financial advisor should be aware of the varying arguments for the treatment of pass-through entities in valuation. The assumptions used to value these entities in a transaction need to be consistent with the facts and application and disclosed to the fiduciary.

7.3.2 Net Operating Losses

A target's net operating losses (NOLs) may have value to the buyer in a proposed transaction. It is important to note that restrictions are placed on the use of NOLs conveyed in transactions. In a sale of the assets of a business, the seller of the business may apply any existing NOLs to offset the gain on sale of the assets. Because the business ceases to exist from a tax perspective once the buyer acquires it, the seller's unused NOLs may "go away" after the acquisition.

The buyer of a corporation with NOLs may continue to utilize them as a carry-forward, subject to certain restrictions. In 1986, Section 382 was enacted into the Internal Revenue Code to limit businesses from being purchased just for their NOLs. The new rules established a limit on the annual tax benefit from NOLs that may be utilized by acquiring firms. This annual limit was calculated as the BEV of the target multiplied by the adjusted federal long-term tax-exempt rate (AFR).

The applications and limitations of NOLs must be considered in properly assessing the value and opining on the fairness of a transaction from a financial point of view. Without such considerations, the results of a valuation exercise would be flawed and the differences in values significant.

7.3.3 Asset Basis

A corporation that purchases the assets of another business is entitled to increase the tax basis of the purchased assets to their fair market values. The corporation is then entitled to deduct additional depreciation and amortization from its income each year for these "stepped-up" assets. While this may be a beneficial position for the buyer of a business, it may not be the case for the individual seller. A seller of assets must treat capital asset appreciation as "ordinary" gains to the extent of prior depreciation. Gains on sale of stock are generally capital gains or could be a nontaxable transaction. Sellers prefer to lower capital gains tax rates or the zero tax of nontaxable transactions.

In the case in which a buyer purchases the equity of a business, there is no change in asset basis and the price does not generate additional amortization or tax shield. The tax law provides an election under IRC Section 338 for the transaction to be treated as an asset sale/purchase. Under IRC Section 338, the buyer must pay the taxes for the gain on the sale of the business, based on the target entity's basis in the assets.

In using the underlying assets approach in valuing the subject business, the impact of the proposed transaction structure must be considered on the basis of the assets. If evaluating a proposed transaction where no step-up in income tax basis is contemplated, the values indicated for the underlying assets must reflect carry-over basis; this requires adjustment to the results indicated from traditional application of asset valuation approaches.

7.3.4 Tax Credits

Other carry-over tax assets may exist, such as foreign tax credits. The independent financial advisor will need to consider these in the fairness opinion analysis.

7.4 INTERNATIONAL BUSINESS CONSIDERATIONS

7.4.1 Foreign Exchange

In opining on the fairness of a transaction involving entities exposed to exchange rate movements, the independent financial advisor must consider the impact of these movements on risk and the value of the business. Exposure to exchange rate movements most often occurs if the business is a multinational organization with subsidiaries doing business in various foreign currencies. More subtly, exposure occurs if the business is purely a domestic operation exposed to significant competition by overseas businesses impacted by foreign exchange developments that may alter the competitive landscape.

Exposure to exchange rate movements should be properly incorporated in the valuation models used to price a business both in terms of consistency in the technical measurement of currency translated cash flows and in terms of risk.

The foreign currency exposure in a business can be accounted for by projecting future currency exchange rates based on international corporate finance theory and actual market data regarding rate movements.

In cases involving significant exchange rate/currency risk, the effects of exchange rate shocks on the value of the enterprise should be evaluated. However, measuring the impact of exchange rate movements on a multi-currency long-term cash flow forecast is a complicated issue. It incorporates factors such as changes in real exchange rates versus changes in nominal rates, price elasticity, their impact on and relationship to commodity prices, production costs, and capital investments. Assessing and quantifying the impact of these factors is complicated by the range of actions taken in response to exchange rate movements by a company's management and other market players.

7.4.2 Multinational Operating Considerations

Operating risks that should be considered by the independent financial advisor when analyzing multinational companies include situations where local regulations, tariffs, and customs are factors that could have a material impact on the financial and operating condition of the subject business. The value of an enterprise with material foreign assets should reflect the income repatriation restrictions imposed on those assets. Therefore, it is important for the independent financial advisor to have some view on these exposures, and a process for incorporating these views into the analysis and the communications with the fiduciary body.

7.4.3 Global Cost of Capital

One of the factors that may confront the independent financial advisor is a local or regional variation to the general cost of capital analysis. Some models used rely on assumptions about markets that are increasingly difficult to support. For example, some cost of capital constructs rely on an assumption of segregated markets that do not reflect the influence of global capital market developments. For a more detailed discussion of developing discount rates from a global perspective, refer to Appendix V.

7.4.4 Foreign Taxes

Recognizing the effect that taxes and tax regulations may have on transaction values is vital in reflecting the underlying fairness of the economics of the transaction. This is especially applicable where multiple tax authorities are involved. Appropriate expertise should be consulted.

NOTES

1. *Eisenberg v. Chicago Milwaukee Corp.*, 538 A.2d at 1057 (Del. Ch. 1988).
2. *Eisenberg*, at 1062.
3. *Jebwab v. MGM Grand Hotels, Inc.*, 509 A.2d at 592.594 (Del. Ch. 1986).
4. *Eisenberg*, at 1060.

5. Although the fiduciary duties of directors are generally considered to be to the shareholders of a business, there are several cases in which courts have extended these duties to the debt holders of the business, even when the business was considered to be solvent.

6. Lease, McConnell, and Mikkelson, "The Market Value of Control In Publicly Traded Corporations," *Journal of Financial Economics* 11, 1983 and "The Market Value of Differential Voting Rights In Closely Held Corporations," *Journal of Business* 57, 1984; Levy, "Economic Evaluation of Voting Power of Common Stock," *Journal of Finance* 38(1), 1982; O'Shea and Siwicki, "Stock Price Premiums for Voting Rights Attributable to Minority Interests," *Business Valuation Review,* December 1991; Jog and Riding, "Price Effects of Dual-Class Shares," *Financial Analysts Journal,* Jan-Feb 1986; Maynes, "Takeover Rights and the Value of Restricted Shares," *Journal of Financial Research* 25(2), 1996; Rydqvist, "Dual-Class Shares—A Review," *Oxford Review of Economic Policy* 8(3), 1992; Megginson, "Restricted Voting Stock, Acquisition Premiums, and the Market for Corporate Control," *Financial Review* 25, 1990; Horner, "The Value of the Corporate Voting Right: Evidence from Switzerland," *Journal of Banking and Finance* 12, 1988; Rydqvist, "Takeover Bids and the Relative Prices of Shares That Differ In Their Voting Rights," *Journal of Banking and Finance* 20, 1996.

7. *Bernard Mandelbaum, et al. v. Commissioner of Internal Revenue* (T.C. Memo 1995-255, June 12, 1995).

8. *Gross v. Commissioner of Internal Revenue,* 272 F.3d 333, (6th Cir. 2001).

9. In *Radiology Associates, Inc.,* 611 A.2d 485; 1991 (Del. Court of Chancery, November 1, 1991).

Bibliography of Select Sources Addressing the Topic of Corporate Governance

The references provided below are intended for general guidance only.

Margaret M. Blair, *Ownership and Control: Rethinking Corporate Governance for the Twenty-First Century* (Washington: Brookings Institution Press, 1995)

George Dallas, *Governance and Risk* (New York: McGraw-Hill Companies, 2004)

Ada Demb and Franz-Fredrick Neubauer, *The Corporate Board: Confronting the Paradoxes* (New York: Oxford University Press, 1992)

Janet Dine, *The Governance of Corporate Groups* (Cambridge: Cambridge University Press, 2000)

Edward Jay Epstein, *Who Owns the Corporation* (New York: Twentieth Century Fund: Priority Press, 1986)

John Kenneth Galbraith, *American Capitalism: The Concept of Countervailing Power* (Boston: Houghton Mifflin Company, 1956)

William Lazonick and Mary O'Sullivan, *Corporate Governance and Sustainable Prosperity* (New York: Palgrave Macmillan, 2002)

Paul Macavoy and Ira M. Millstein, *The Recurrent Crisis in Corporate Governance* (New York: Palgrave Macmillan Ltd., 2004)

Robert A.G. Monks and Nell Minow, *Corporate Governance* (Cambridge, Massachusetts: Basil Blackwell, Inc., 1995)

Walter J. Salmon, et al., *Harvard Business Review on Corporate Governance* (Cambridge, Massachusetts: Harvard Business School Press, 2000)

Disclosure Requirement Summary Under Rule 13e3

United States
Securities and Exchange Commission
Washington, D.C. 20549

SCHEDULE 13E-3 EXCERPT

§240.13e-100.

Schedule 13E-3 [§240.13e-3], Rule 13e-3 Transaction Statement Pursuant to Section 13(e) of the Securities Exchange Act of 1934 and Rule 13e-3 [§240.13e-3] thereunder.

Item 8. Fairness of the Transaction.

Furnish the information required by Item 1014 of Regulation M-A (§229.1014 of this chapter).

§229.1014 (Item 1014) Fairness of the going-private transaction

a. *Fairness*. State whether the subject company or affiliate filing the statement reasonably believes that the Rule 13e-3 transaction is fair or unfair to unaffiliated security holders. If any director dissented to or abstained from voting on the Rule 13e-3 transaction, identify the director, and indicate, if known, after making reasonable inquiry, the reasons for the dissent or abstention.

b. *Factors considered in determining fairness*. Discuss in reasonable detail the material factors upon which the belief stated in paragraph (a) of this section is based and, to the extent practicable, the weight assigned to each factor. The discussion must include an analysis of the extent, if any, to which the filing person's beliefs are based on the factors described in Instruction 2 of this section, paragraphs (c), (d), and (e) of this section and Item 1015 of Regulation M-A (§229.1015).

c. *Approval of security holders.* State whether or not the transaction is structured so that approval of at least a majority of unaffiliated security holders is required.

d. *Unaffiliated representative.* State whether or not a majority of directors who are not employees of the subject company has retained an unaffiliated representative to act solely on behalf of unaffiliated security holders for purposes of negotiating the terms of the Rule 13e-3 transaction and/or preparing a report concerning the fairness of the transaction.

e. *Approval of directors.* State whether or not the Rule 13e-3 transaction was approved by a majority of the directors of the subject company who are not employees of the subject company.

f. *Other offers.* If any offer of the type described in paragraph (viii) of Instruction 2 to this section has been received, describe the offer and state the reasons for its rejection.

Instructions to Item 1014:

1. A statement that the issuer or affiliate has no reasonable belief as to the fairness of the Rule 13e-3 transaction to unaffiliated security holders will not be considered sufficient disclosure in response to paragraph (a) of this section.

2. The factors that are important in determining the fairness of a transaction to unaffiliated security holders and the weight, if any, that should be given to them in a particular context will vary. Normally such factors will include, among others, those referred to in paragraphs (c), (d) and (e) of this section and whether the consideration offered to unaffiliated security holders constitutes fair value in relation to:
   (i)   Current market prices;
   (ii)   Historical market prices;
   (iii) Net book value;
   (iv)   Going concern value;

(v)   Liquidation value;

(vi)   Purchase prices paid in previous purchases disclosed in response to Item 1002(f) of Regulation M-A (§229.1002(f));

(vii)   Any report, opinion, or appraisal described in Item 1015 of Regulation M-A (§229.1015); and

(viii) Firm offers of which the subject company or affiliate is aware made by any unaffiliated person, other than the filing persons, during the past two years for:

   (A)   The merger or consolidation of the subject company with or into another company, or *vice versa*;

   (B)   The sale or other transfer of all or any substantial part of the assets of the subject company; or

   (C)   A purchase of the subject company's securities that would enable the holder to exercise control of the subject company.

3. Conclusory statements, such as "The Rule 13e-3 transaction is fair to unaffiliated security holders in relation to net book value, going concern value and future prospects of the issuer" will not be considered sufficient disclosure in response to paragraph (b) of this section.

Sample Generic Information Request List

The material provided below is intended for general guidance only.

The following is a preliminary list of information requests relevant to our analysis of *ABC Company* ("ABC" or the "Company") as of a current date (the "Valuation Date"). We understand that all of the data requested below may not be available. We will review the data that is available, and if necessary, discuss possible alternatives with you. Please contact *Name* at *(000) 000-0000* if you have any questions or comments.

A. HISTORY AND NATURE OF THE COMPANY

1. Discussion of the history and operations of the Company, including major milestones and current nature of the business.

2. Copies of Company brochures or literature that describe the Company and its products/services. Please include any sales/promotional materials supplied to prospective customers.

3. List of subsidiaries and significant interest in other companies.

4. Assess the Company's competitive position within the market now and in the future.

5. List the major shareholders of the Company, as of the Valuation Date, including shares held (by class) and a discussion of the effective voting rights and other attributes of each class.

6. List all actual and proposed (current or past) transactions involving the Company's stock. Include number of shares, type of transaction (third-party sale, related-party sale, etc.), price of the transaction, the manner in which the price was determined (arm's length negotiation, appraisal, etc.), and any other transaction-specific information that is available.

7. List all actual and proposed (current or past) transactions involving the Company's assets and/or operating subsidiaries. Include purchase price, type of transaction, the manner in which

the price was determined (arm's length negotiation, appraisal, etc.), and any other transaction-specific information that is available.

8. Details of any previous offers or discussions to buy/sell the Company or any of its operating subsidiaries.

9. Articles of incorporation, bylaws (including amendments), LLC formation agreement(s), management agreements, etc.

10. List senior managers of the Company, including position, age, salary, bonuses, years in industry, and years with the Company.

B. PRODUCTS AND MARKETS

1. Discuss the pricing of the products/services.

2. Discuss the impact of new products/services and/or competing technologies on the Company's products/services.

3. Discuss the growth prospects for the Company's products/ services by major market.

C. SALES AND MARKETING

1. Describe the Company's marketing activities, including methods of generating new customers and sale of additional products/services to existing customers.

2. Discuss the size and structure of the Company's sales force, including both in-house and independent sales representatives.

3. Provide a copy of the Company's marketing plan, including advertising media and budgets.

D. FINANCIAL INFORMATION

1. Audited [or unaudited] financial information (balance sheets, income statements, and cash flow statements) for the last three years, including any information on net operating loss carry-forwards (NOLs) and any limitation on the use of NOLs, if applicable, for each operating subsidiary.

2. Latest interim financial statements (which will be assumed to be as of the Valuation Date). Please include interim statements

for the prior year's "latest interim period" (i.e., if the first three months of this fiscal year are provided, also provide the first three months for the prior year) for each operating subsidiary.

3. Identify any nonrecurring or special accounting items that had a material impact on the Company's performance, by operating subsidiary, by year.

4. Provide details on any intercompany transactions.

5. Pro-forma income statement and balance sheet showing the Company's annual projected revenues, expenses, and balance sheet positions over its forecast period. Please separately identify or itemize interest, depreciation, and amortization expenses. In addition, please include price, volume, and customer retention assumptions for each year of the explicit forecast.

6. Projected capital expenditures and working capital (i.e., Days Payable, Days Receivable, Days Inventory, Prepaids, Accruals, etc.) required to support the projected growth in revenues.

7. Any recent business plans and documents regarding the products and operations of the Company, including its products and services, markets, and competitors.

8. Any material opportunities (i.e., new product launches) that the Company is considering and that have not been factored into the projections.

9. Identification of any nonoperating income or assets such as excess land, facilities, equipment, or marketable securities.

10. Identification of any contingent or off-balance-sheet assets or liabilities (pending lawsuits, compliance requirements, leasehold interests, other contingencies, etc.).

11. If not disclosed in the financial statements, provide details on what is classified in "Other Expenses," "Other Assets," and "Other Liabilities."

12. List of significant customer relationships, supplier relationships, contracts, patents, copyrights, trademarks, and other intangible assets.

13. Amounts and dates of any dividend distributions (if not included on the financial statements).

14. Describe any significant benefits and perquisites received by shareholders, officers, or management of the Company or its subsidiaries.

15. List any significant personal expenses of shareholders, officers, or managers that have been paid by the Company.

16. Describe any significant differences in the accounting for tax and book purposes for the Company.

17. Provide statements of accounts receivable with aging as of the Valuation Date if not detailed in the financial statements.

E. COMPETITION

1. List and describe each of the Company's competitors. Provide details on company size, market share, and products/services offered in each of the Company's markets.

2. Discuss the competitive nature of the market (i.e., do companies compete on the basis of price, quality, service, etc.?).

3. Is there a dominant business/competitive strategy among the successful firms? Is this model currently changing/evolving and how?

F. FACILITIES

1. List the Company's major facilities, including locations, brief descriptions of their size and layout, function, limitations, if any, and whether they are owned or leased. Include original cost, net book values, and approximate ages, if known.

2. Describe any property, plant, or equipment owned by the Company that is not presently used in the Company's operations. Include original cost and approximate fair market value, if known.

3. Provide any available market value information for fixed assets, such as previous real or personal property appraisals, insurance appraisals, earlier offers to purchase the property or assets, etc.

G. GOVERNMENT REGULATION

1. Assess the regulation of the subject entity, customers, and suppliers by local, state, and federal regulatory authorities and the effect on costs and Company growth.

2. Identify any changes in governmental regulations (existing or pending) that may significantly impact the financial performance of the Company.

H. TECHNOLOGY

1. Describe the current technology utilized in the Company's operations.
2. Discuss new technologies being implemented and their potential impact on the Company's operations.

I. OTHER

1. Reports of any appraisals or valuations performed relating to the determination of transaction prices or opinions of value for the Company's stock or its assets.
2. Any existing buy-sell agreements, options to purchase stock, or rights of first refusal.
3. Copies of any shareholder agreements or agreements relating to the transfer of the Company's stock (preferred or common).
4. Copies of all significant contracts or leases to which the Company is or has been a party during the past two years.

Sample Risk Assessment and Due Diligence Questions

The material provided below is intended for general guidance only.

MANAGEMENT AND PRINCIPAL OWNERS

a. There is information (e.g., a person's conviction for a criminal offense or suspension or sanction by a regulatory body) that calls into question the integrity of one or more members of the senior management, or otherwise raises questions as to the advisor's ability to rely on the management's representations.

b. An individual with no apparent ownership interest in, or executive position with, the company appears to exercise substantial influence over its affairs.

c. A significant or unexpected change of management has recently occurred or is likely to occur in the next year.

d. There is any other reason to question the ethics or business methods of the company or its board members or its key management.

e. The management has become unreasonably demanding of the advisor's personnel and has become difficult to work with, or has placed unreasonable time constraints for the issuance of the advisor's reports.

f. A single individual dominates the management in a manner that inhibits or precludes the effectiveness of others (for example, other board members) in performing their duties.

g. There has been an unusual turnover rate of individuals in key positions.

h. There has been a high turnover rate of professional advisors, including audit firms, and/or there is evidence of disputes with professional advisors, including audit firms.

i. The management places undue emphasis on achieving planned results and/or issues overly optimistic forecasts.

j. The management is willing to take unusually high risks in areas affecting the financial position (e.g., credit control policies, research and development projects, compliance with laws and regulations).

k. A significant part of directors' remuneration is derived from bonuses or stock options or other remuneration linked to earnings or share price.

l. The management has disposed of a large part of its shares in the company in the past year, or plans to do so.

m. The management has failed to appoint reputable professional advisors (e.g., attorneys, investment bankers, accountants) appropriate to the company's needs.

n. Significant internal control recommendations are not being addressed or implemented by the management.

o. There is a lack of concern by the senior management over a weak internal accounting control system.

p. Key management and/or members of the board of directors have apparent conflicts of interest with respect to the buyer or an affiliate of the buyer.

LEGALITY OF ACTIVITIES AND REPUTATION

a. A substantial part of the company's income and expenses comprise commissions or fees for which there is little or no supporting documentation.

b. There are significant unexplained cash flows between the company and other companies incorporated abroad from which the company itself does not profit.

c. The company's management appears to act on instructions from persons whose identities are deliberately kept secret.

d. The company is unduly secretive about the nature of its customer base.

BUSINESS ENVIRONMENT

a. The company operates in an industry that is experiencing or is likely to experience an abnormal number of business failures or other conditions (e.g., takeover rumors) that could cause its accounting and reporting practices to be scrutinized by third parties at a later date.

b. If publicly traded, the price of the company's shares has changed significantly in comparison with similar companies in the same industry, or there has been an unusually high trading volume.

c. There are matters such as significant litigation between this company and another client of the advisor that could cause the advisor to have a conflict of interest.

d. The company has recently taken legal action against other advisors.

e. The company's accounts are likely to be used in litigation or other claims.

f. The company has been criticized by a regulatory authority in respect of its activities or its accounting and reporting standards.

FINANCIAL POSITION AND PROSPECTS

a. The company has experienced, or expects to experience, a severe adverse business development that could result in reporting or business risks that would be unacceptable, even though taken into account in the valuation.

b. It is unlikely that the company will be able to meet its financial obligations as they become due.

c. The company has substantial debt from unusual sources (e.g., related parties) or on unusual terms.

d. The company has employed aggressive or "creative" accounting policies to improve earnings and/or degree of leverage.

e. The company's performance has been significantly better or worse than that of its industry as a whole, and the reason is not apparent.

f. The company has grown by making acquisitions, and is dependent on further acquisitions to meet the market's expectations of future growth.

    g. The company's method of accounting for acquisitions has enabled it to show high growth when real growth was low.

    h. A major portion of the company's revenue is dependent on a single customer or group of customers whose continued business is in doubt because of adverse business conditions or competition from others.

    i. The company has significant joint venture agreements with third parties who may be in financial difficulties.

REPORTING ENVIRONMENT

    a. The company engages in transactions with companies under common control or with other related parties that are not being investigated or reported on by the advisor and that can be expected to present significant unusual risks to the advisor.

    b. Formal or informal restrictions have been placed on the advisor that limit the advisor's ability to communicate effectively with nonexecutive directors or other directors having responsibilities for overseeing the company's operations.

    c. Audit reports have been qualified.

    d. Audits have led to significant adjustments to the accounts or significant weaknesses in systems being reported to the management.

    e. The advisor would be relying on other firms for material parts of the advisor's work; for example, if the company has had significant excess real estate and the appraisal is not performed by the advisor.

    f. There are significant related parties or associated companies with which significant transactions may occur, and to which the advisor will not have access or that have different year-ends.

    g. There is reason to believe that the advisor will not be able to render a satisfactory report because of such matters as scope limitations, going concern problems, significant litigation, or accounting issues.

    h. The advisor is aware of recent "opinion shopping" by management.

    i. There are restrictions on the disclosure of ownership or identity of shareholders.

j. The company's accounting records or internal control systems are inadequate or in poor condition.

k. The company's directors include persons (e.g., stockbrokers or attorneys) who also act for the company in a professional capacity that could lead to conflicts of interest for the directors concerned.

l. The company maintains banking relationships with a number of different banks for no apparent reason.

m. There has been a significant change in the management or ownership of the company during the year.

n. The company engages in unique, highly complex, and material transactions that pose difficult "substance over form" questions, especially investing in "derivatives."

o. The management has a history of completing significant or unusual transactions late in the company's financial year.

p. During the period covered by relevant financial statements, a relatively small number of transactions have had a material effect on results, and such transactions were designed to meet the minimum criteria required to be met to permit revenue to be recognized (creative accounting).

q. There are special problems relating to accounting estimates, or measurements that are of unusual significance because of the nature of the industry or the relative importance of the accounts.

r. The company uses accounting policies that are inconsistent with predominant industry practice or are otherwise questionable.

s. A change to what might be a less appropriate accounting policy has recently been made or is under active consideration (particularly where the company is contemplating a public offering of its shares or is raising money by other means).

t. There are significant nonmonetary transactions.

u. The company carries significant "off-balance-sheet" financing liabilities.

TRANSACTION CIRCUMSTANCES

a. The advisor is brought into the transaction at a very late stage.

b. It appears that the effort to reach potential bidders was insufficient.

c. There is an absence of logical potential bidders.

d. Communication is entirely with management and not the board.

e. The selling shareholder group has been contentious or litigious as to indicate a significant likelihood of litigation by a dissatisfied faction of shareholders.

f. For any reason, the negotiation of the deal price appears to be not arm's length (e.g., the buyer has the ability to force or otherwise control or influence the seller's decision regarding the sale).

g. The parties to the transaction are not truly independent (e.g., related-party transaction).

h. The party indemnifying the advisor will not survive or will lack sufficient funds to honor the indemnification.

i. Opinion is being used "offensively" (i.e., to convince minority shareholders to undertake an action such as approving a merger).

j. Opinion is being used in a situation where no board or other fiduciary is recommending the transaction.

k. Opinion is being used in a higher risk transaction like a real estate partnership roll-up or bankruptcy situation.

l. Opinion is to be publicly disclosed via proxy statement, registration statement, or otherwise, or is likely to receive press coverage.

m. The marketing of the company or security has been significantly restricted so as to call into question whether a more favorable offer could be achieved with appropriate marketing.

n. The transaction offer to the company provides different proceeds for minority shareholders.

o. The transaction offer received by the company is accompanied by significant levels of payments for noncompetition, possible excessive salaries or expected bonuses for management (especially if also majority shareholders).

OTHER ISSUES

The key to the opinion process is stating precisely the circumstances on which the advisor must opine. Defining the engagement is a critical phase of the job. The values of companies and their securities are always dependent on the specific situation. Before an assignment can begin, the following questions must be answered:

1. What is being valued (minority interest, etc.)?
2. What is the date of the opinion?
3. What is being received in exchange (e.g., cash, securities, other property, contingent payments)?
4. What is the standard of valuation and how is it applied? This will differ from state to state.
5. What are the limitations imposed, if any? (For example, has the "market" for the company or security been restricted? Has there been an appropriate effort to solicit interest among enough logical potential acquirers?)

Cost of Capital Discussion

The material provided below is intended for illustrative purposes only.

In the application of the discounted cash flow methodology, the projected expected cash flows and terminal value of the subject company are converted to their respective present value equivalent using a rate of return that reflects the risk of an investment in the capital of the business, as well as the time value of money. This return is an overall rate based upon the expected individual rates of return for invested capital (equity and interest-bearing debt). This return, known as the WACC, is calculated by weighting the required returns on interest-bearing debt and common equity capital in proportion to their estimated percentages in an assumed optimal or actual expected capital structure.

The textbook formula for calculating the WACC is:

$$WACC = [Kd \times d\%] + [Ke \times e\%]$$

where:

WACC = Weighted average rate of return on invested capital
Kd = After-tax rate of return on debt capital
d% = Debt capital as a percentage of the sum of the debt and common equity capital (Total Invested Capital)
Ke = Rate of return on common equity capital
e% = Common equity capital as a percentage of the Total Invested Capital

The rate of return on debt capital is the rate a prudent debt investor would require on interest-bearing debt at today's interest rates given the credit risk of the business. Since the interest expense on debt capital employed is deductible for income tax purposes, an analysis should be performed of the subject company's ability to deduct interest expense and take advantage of the resulting income tax shield benefit. In its simplest form, the benefits of the interest expense tax shield can be factored into the WACC calculation through the use of an after-tax interest rate in the calculation, which is calculated as follows:

$$Kd = K \times (1 - T_c)$$

where:

Kd = After-tax rate of return on debt capital

K = Pretax rate of return on debt capital

T_c = Effective corporate income tax rate

One of the problems with this textbook approach is that it assumes that the impact of the deduction of interest expense will result in a tax benefit in the period in which the interest is paid; this simplifying assumption often is not realistic. Any delay in the tax benefit effectively increases the cost of capital.

The rate of return on equity capital is more difficult to estimate. The Capital Asset Pricing Model (CAPM) is one of the most widely used models for estimating the required return on equity. While the textbook CAPM is widely accepted for the purpose of estimating a company's required return on equity capital,[1] the accuracy of the textbook CAPM has failed many empirical tests.

In applying the CAPM, the rate of return on common equity is estimated as the current risk-free rate of return indicated by an appropriate instrument, plus an equity premium expected over the risk-free rate of return multiplied by the "beta" for the business subject to analysis (i.e., a risk-adjusted equity premium).

Practical application of a CAPM-based model relies on an estimate of the equity premium for the market as a whole. Since the expectations of the average investor are not directly observable, the equity premium must be inferred using one of several methods.[2]

Beta is defined as a risk measure that reflects the sensitivity of an asset's value to the movements of a relevant market, or portfolio of assets, as a whole.

Beta is a statistical measure of the covariance of returns of a specific asset with returns on a diversified portfolio of assets. Hence, beta is regarded as a measure of the market's perception of the relative risk of the subject business or asset. Practical application of the CAPM is dependent upon the ability to identify publicly traded companies that have similar risk characteristics as the subject business (i.e., guideline companies), in order to derive meaningful market-derived indications of the appropriate beta to incorporate into the analysis.

While the textbook CAPM holds that beta is the market's sole risk measure, empirical tests of CAPM have shown that measurement problems exist with beta estimation techniques commonly used by data services, and that beta alone may not capture the market's pricing of risk for "small players" in an industry.

Accurate beta estimation requires consideration of inefficiencies in market reaction to economic developments. The independent financial advisor should not rely solely on published beta sources; rather, he or she should use several beta estimation models and benchmark the results to characteristics of fundamental industry risks. In addition, an adjustment may be appropriate to account for the relative small size of the subject company. On average, smaller companies (i.e., smaller players in an industry) are more risky than larger companies, and empirical studies have shown that beta often underestimates this added risk. Remember, one is assessing the risk of the subject investment (i.e., subject business), not the risk of an acquiring company.

Betas derived from publicly traded stocks and as commonly reported in published sources are "levered," which means they reflect the added risk to equity investors associated with debt financing in the capital structure of the subject company (they reflect both operating and financial risks). To derive a beta applicable to a subject company based on guideline public companies, the reported levered betas of the guideline companies must first be "unlevered" to remove the effects of financial risks of the guideline companies. Unlevered betas are also known as operating or asset betas. One then "relevers" the beta at the appropriate debt to total capital levels for the subject company.

In estimating the cost of equity capital, the independent financial advisor needs to go beyond simply applying the textbook CAPM. For example, the empirically derived *Risk Premium Report* [3] allows one to estimate risk-adjusted equity premiums using several methodologies based on risks of the subject company (e.g., relative size as measured by revenues and net income, operating margin and variability of operating margin). The resultant cost of equity capital estimates derived from various sources should be correlated before a conclusion is reached.

In estimating the cost of equity capital, a practical model is:

Ke = Rf + Risk-adjusted equity premium + Specific risk adjustments

where:
Rf = Risk-free rate as of valuation date

Lastly, an estimate of the appropriate capital structure is typically based on observing proportions of interest-bearing debt, preferred equity, and common equity of publicly traded companies in similar lines of business as the subject company.

GLOBAL CONSIDERATIONS

While the cost of capital is constituted from both the cost of equity and the cost of debt, it is the estimation of the cost of equity that presents challenges in the international context. Increased globalization broadens the definition of the market for all investors. The CAPM framework should be broadened when valuing multinational companies, and it is known as the global or international CAPM approach.

Unlike the textbook CAPM that calculates the cost of equity based on a domestic risk-free rate, the domestic equity premium and a beta that measures covariance with respect to the domestic equity market, the global CAPM essentially measures all of the variables, assuming there is a global supply and global demand for all the different forms of capital.

Estimation of the global equity premium is less straightforward. Practitioners agree that the equity premium is a forward-looking concept, though many use historical data to measure it. In measuring the equity premium for fair value purposes, the intent is not to make forecasts of the stock market or to predict the future. Rather, the goal is to measure as objectively as possible the expectations of the average investor. Because this expectation is not readily observable, the equity premium must be estimated by one of several techniques.

One approach is to use the average premium that investors have historically earned over and above the returns on a perceived risk-free instrument. The premium obtained using historical return data is sensitive to the time period over which one calculates the average. Depending on the time period chosen, the historical approach yields an average premium in established markets ranging from 5 to 8 percent.

An alternative is to use a forward-looking approach. There are a number of forward-looking methods available. One option is to use the expected returns implied by a dividend discount model calculation for a large sample of public companies. Another option is to use the average expected return obtained from a survey of investment analysts who follow the equity markets. Again, this approach will lead to differing estimates, depending on the source, and results can range from 3 to 7 percent.

Furthermore, if this analysis is performed in a global context, additional factors need to be considered. In the context of a global CAPM framework, an equity premium is sought for a global investment index rather than an index representative of the local equity market. However, the United States represents the largest fraction of the global stock market. Moreover, the U.S. market is comprised of many globally diversified companies that together represent substantial exposures to the rest of the world, including emerging markets. Finally, many nominally U.S. equities are traded abroad, and vice versa: Many foreign companies now have U.S. listings. For these reasons, it would be surprising if returns on the U.S. and global portfolios diverged substantially for extended periods.

Beta estimates in this context need to measure covariance with respect to the global market portfolio. For practical application, one widely accepted proxy for the global market portfolio is given by the Morgan Stanley Capital International Index (MSCI Index). Estimates of global betas are determined by substituting the MSCI Index as the relevant benchmark index. Because many developing markets are not highly correlated with more mature markets, betas measured with respect to the MSCI Index are typically lower than betas calculated with respect to Organization for Economic Cooperation and Development (OECD) type markets. This resulting uncorrelated nature of many developing markets means that international investment diversifies the investor against some domestic systematic risk.

The global market is dominated (in market value terms) by industrial countries with overall risk characteristics similar to those of the United States. Therefore, a risk-adjusted equity premium derived from U.S. data is often considered a reasonable proxy for a global risk-adjusted equity premium. Even if one does not adhere to a global CAPM approach, it is still expected that the required return for companies with similar risk characteristics in different developed countries will be roughly equal to each other due to the ability of investors to move funds between countries.

Presently, consideration of historical and forward-looking sources mentioned above typically leads to the conclusion that a reasonable estimate of the equity premium is in the 4 to 6 percent range. Estimates of global risk-adjusted equity premiums (unlevered) for various industries are published in the *Global Cost of Capital Report*. [4]

NOTES

1. W. F. Sharpe, *Investments* (Englewood Cliffs, New Jersey, Prentice Hall, 1985).

2. For example, see "The Equity Risk Premium," Roger Grabowski and David King, Chapter 1 in *The Handbook of Business Valuation and Intellectual Property Analysis* (New York: McGraw-Hill, 2004).

3. Standard & Poor's Corporate Value Consulting Risk Premium Report, published annually, www.ibbotson.com

4. Global Cost of Capital Report, published quarterly, www.standardandpoors.com

Biographies for Contributing Authors

MICHAEL G. ATHANASON

Michael G. Athanason is Managing Director for Standard & Poor's Corporate Value Consulting group, based in New York, and Global Product Leader of the Corporate Finance Consulting group, a position he assumed in May 2004. In his position, Mr. Athanason specializes in Transaction Advisory Services, Financial Engineering, Fairness Opinions, Financial and Strategic Modeling, and Capital Structure. Mr. Athanason has more than 20 years of energy industry and corporate finance experience. Prior to joining Standard & Poor's, he was Corporate Finance Energy & Utilities Industry Leader at Ernst & Young. Mr. Athanason specializes in corporate finance work, including mergers, acquisitions, corporate divestures, financial restructuring, strategic planning, and business valuation, as well as developing international market entry strategies for U.S. and European companies. Mr. Athanason holds a B.S. degree in Ocean Engineering from the Florida Institute of Technology and an MBA from Georgetown University.

CHARLES A. BAKER

Charles A. Baker is a partner in the New York office of the law firm of Paul, Hastings, Janofsky & Walker LLP. His business law practice focuses on all aspects of corporate finance, mergers and acquisitions, securities, and private equity matters. Mr. Baker has extensive transactional experience representing both U.S. and non-U.S. entities in mergers and acquisitions, including auctioned dispositions, unsolicited and negotiated tender offers for public and private corporations and partnerships, leveraged buyouts, and proxy contests. Mr. Baker has developed specific experience representing public accounting firms, consulting firms, and investment banks on corporate finance advisory matters, including the establishment and provision of fairness opinion services. He has lectured extensively on these matters to various groups including: The Investment Program

Association, The Wharton School of the University of Pennsylvania, and private seminar organizations. Mr. Baker currently serves as an executive officer and on the board of trustees of the Leukemia & Lymphoma Society. He is a member of the New York Bar and the American Bar Association, where he serves on the Business Law Committee and the Association of the Bar of the City of New York. Previously, he served as a staff intern for former Senator Bill Bradley. Mr. Baker holds a B.A degree, magna cum laude, in Political Science from the University of Rochester in 1982. He holds a J.D. degree from Cornell Law School in 1985, where he served as a member of the Moot Court Board and taught undergraduate business law.

NATALIA V. BRUSLANOVA

Natalia V. Bruslanova is a former Manager in the Corporate Value Consulting group of Standard & Poor's, based in New York. Her particular focus on corporate finance consulting was in capital structure and fairness opinions. Prior to joining Standard & Poor's in 2001, Ms. Bruslanova spent three years with the PricewaterhouseCoopers Corporate Finance practice in London and one year with the Price Waterhouse Management Consulting Services group in Kiev, Ukraine. She holds a B.A. in Economics from the University of Kiev-Mohyla Academy in Ukraine and an M.Sc. in International Accounting and Finance from the London School of Economics and Political Science. Ms. Bruslanova also holds a Chartered Financial Analyst (CFA) designation.

PHILIP J. CLEMENTS

Philip J. Clements is retired (2004) Executive Vice President, Standard & Poor's Corporate Value Consulting group. Mr. Clements was formerly Global Leader, Corporate Value Consulting, at PricewaterhouseCoopers LLP, and was U.S. Leader, Corporate Finance, for one of its predecessor firm Coopers & Lybrand. He was a Board Member and Finance Committee member of both PricewaterhouseCoopers and Coopers & Lybrand. In his executive role, Mr. Clements has overseen acquisitions and their integration. In his role as a practicing professional, he advises companies and their boards on corporate strategies and transactions of all sizes. Mr. Clements holds an LLM (Taxation) from New York University School of Law, a J.D. from University of Puget Sound/Seattle University School of Law, and a B.A. in Accounting from the University of Puget Sound.

ROGER J. GRABOWSKI

Roger J. Grabowski, ASA, is a Managing Director in Standard & Poor's Corporate Value Consulting practice. He was formerly a partner of PricewaterhouseCoopers LLP and one of its predecessor firms, Price Waterhouse (where he founded its U.S. Valuation Services practice and managed the real estate appraisal practice). He has directed valuations of businesses, interests in businesses, intellectual property, intangible assets, real property, and machinery and equipment. Mr. Grabowski has testified in court as an expert witness on the value of closely held businesses and business interests, matters of solvency, valuation and amortization of intangible assets, and other valuation issues. His testimony in U.S. District Court was quoted in the U.S. Supreme Court opinion decided in his client's favor in the landmark *Newark Morning Ledger* case. Mr. Grabowski coauthors the annual *S&P Corporate Value Consulting Risk Premium Report*, published at www.ibbotson.com. He publishes regularly, and coauthored three chapters in the recently released *The Handbook of Business Valuation and Intellectual Property Analysis* (McGraw-Hill, 2004). Mr. Grabowski teaches courses for the American Society of Appraisers, including the Cost of Capital, which he codeveloped as part of the curriculum of the Center for Advanced Valuation Studies. He holds a BBA degree in Finance from Loyola University of Chicago and completed all course work in the Doctoral Program in Finance from Northwestern University in Chicago.

ALICIA GROSMAN

Alicia Grosman is a Manager in Standard & Poor's Corporate Value Consulting practice in New York. She has performed numerous valuations of businesses, equity interests, intellectual property, and intangible assets for financial reporting and tax purposes, in the context of mergers and acquisitions. Ms. Grosman has over five years of financial services experience, including three years in the valuation profession. She has assisted clients in a broad array of industries and has significant expertise in the media and entertainment industry. Ms. Grosman holds a B.S. in Accounting and an MBA in Finance and Management from the Leonard N. Stern School of Business at New York University. She is a Certified Public Accountant in the State of New York and a Level III Candidate in the Chartered Financial Analyst program.

JOHN KWON

John Kwon is a Manager in Standard & Poor's Corporate Value Consulting group, based in New York. In this capacity, he has provided corporate finance advice to clients in a variety of industries, including consumer products, technology, media and entertainment, telecommunications, automotive, and pharmaceuticals. Mr. Kwon has focused on providing fairness opinions and other corporate finance advisory services to his clients over the past 10 years. He has also performed numerous valuations, including business enterprise valuations and valuations of intellectual property and intangible assets. He specializes in identifying and quantifying the opportunities and risk inherent in company projections. Prior to joining Standard & Poor's, Mr. Kwon worked for PricewaterhouseCoopers LLP, Alliant Techsystems, Inc., and Honeywell Inc. Mr. Kwon holds an MBA from New York University and a B.S. in Electrical Engineering from Massachusetts Institute of Technology.

KEVIN C. LOGUE

Kevin C. Logue is a partner in the New York office of the law firm of Paul, Hastings, Janofsky, & Walker LLP and specializes in the areas of mergers and acquisitions, securities/shareholder disputes, and financial services litigation. As the Vice Chair of the firm's National Mergers & Acquisitions Practice Group, Mr. Logue regularly counsels and litigates on behalf of boards of directors, special committees, companies and advisors, in a variety of corporate governance and mergers and acquisitions matters, including class action and shareholder derivative litigation matters. Mr. Logue holds a BBA degree from the University of Kentucky and a J.D. degree from St. John's University School of Law, 1984, where he served as editor-in-chief of the *St. John's Law Review*.

SHERRI B. SALTZMAN

Sherri B. Saltzman is a Director in Standard & Poor's Corporate Value Consulting group based in New Jersey. Ms. Saltzman joined Standard & Poor's in September 2001, when the company acquired the U.S. Corporate Value Consulting business from PricewaterhouseCoopers LLP. Prior to her current position as Director of Marketing and Communications for Standard & Poor's Corporate Value Consulting, Ms. Saltzman spent over 10 years performing business and asset valuations for a number of clients.

She holds a B.S. in Accounting from Pennsylvania State University and an MBA in Finance from New York University. Ms. Saltzman is also a Certifed Public Accountant in the State of New Jersey.

YVETTE AUSTIN SMITH

Yvette Austin Smith is a Director in Standard & Poor's Corporate Value Consulting based in New York. She specializes in transaction-related financial opinions—principally, fairness opinions, capital adequacy opinions, and commercial reasonableness opinions—and retrospective solvency opinions. She has more than 11 years of experience in valuing both equity and debt securities and financial portfolios, with a particular emphasis on illiquid securities, private investments, and financial assets in connection with bankruptcy and claims of fraud or price manipulation. Ms. Smith has provided financial opinions for a wide range of corporate transactions and has served as a consulting expert in securities fraud, bankruptcy, and contested M&A litigation matters. Ms. Smith is an Associate Member of the American Bar Association. She is currently providing valuation commentary to a forthcoming revision of the ABA Model Public Company Acquisition Agreement, and contributing to a forthcoming ABA Deal Makers' Dictionary. She is also member of the American Bankruptcy Institute. Ms Smith holds an MBA from Columbia Business School and an A.B. from Harvard University.

PAUL G. TASKER

Paul G. Tasker is a former Manager with Standard & Poor's Corporate Value Consulting and serves as Fairness Opinion Champion for the Philadelphia office. He has extensive experience in the valuation of controlling and minority interests in closely held companies as well as subsidiaries and divisions of public companies, and he has prepared valuations and information memoranda for the purposes of merger, acquisition, and divestiture pricing; deal structuring; fairness opinions; international, federal, and state tax planning; litigation involving shareholder disputes and breach of contract; bankruptcy and financing. In addition, Mr. Tasker has experience in the implementation of SFAS 141 (purchase price allocation analysis and assessment of impact of amortization on EPS) and 142 (goodwill impairment testing); and the valuation of intangible assets, including contracts, patents, trademarks, customer relationships, purchased in-process R&D,

and proprietary technology. During his five years with Standard & Poor's, Mr. Tasker was involved in more than 100 transactions in a wide and diverse field of industries, including, but not limited to, consumer and industrial products, integrated health care, and information technology. He holds a B.S. degree in Business Administration from Villanova University, where he majored in Finance and Management Information Systems.

PHILIP WISLER

Philip Wisler is a Philadelphia-based Managing Director in Standard & Poor's Corporate Value Consulting practice. During his 14 years as a corporate finance consulting practitioner, he has been involved in more than 400 valuation, financial consulting, and buy-side/sell-side advisory projects encompassing a wide range of industries, including financial services, consumer and industrial products manufacturing and distribution, heavy industrial, technology, and integrated health care. Projects managed by Mr. Wisler have been used to facilitate transactions, to support positions of fairness and solvency, and to provide guidance to state and federal regulatory agencies (e.g., State Departments of Insurance, Attorneys General, the Securities and Exchange Commission, state legislators, and the Internal Revenue Service). Mr. Wisler is presently the National Director of Standard & Poor's Corporate Value Consulting practice's fairness opinion service and participates in all fairness opinion projects performed by the firm. He has provided litigation support to clients and has been accepted as an expert by courts in the areas of valuation and fairness opinions. Revenues of clients served by Mr. Wisler have ranged from $25 million to over $6 billion. Mr. Wisler holds a Bachelor of Economics degree in finance from the Wharton School, University of Pennsylvania, and an MBA with concentrations in finance and accounting from Drexel University.

INDEX